Black and Bluenose

The Contemporary History of a Community

Charles Saunders

Pottersfield Press
Lawrencetown Beach
Nova Scotia
Canada

Canadian Cataloguing in Publication Data

Saunders, Charles R.

      Black and Bluenose

      ISBN 1-895900-23-9

1. Black Canadians – Nova Scotia – History. * 2. Blacks – Nova Scotia – History. I. Title.

FC2350.B6S28 1999   971.6'00496   C99-950016-3
F1040.N3S28 1999

Credits:
Cover photo: Tony Caldwell/The Daily News
Inside photos: The Daily News

Pottersfield Press gratefully acknowledges the ongoing support of the Nova Scotia Department of Education, Cultural Affairs Division as well as the Canada Council for the Arts. We acknowledge the financial support of the Government of Canada through the Book Publishing Industry Development Program for our publishing activities.

Pottersfield Press
83 Leslie Road
East Lawrencetown
Nova Scotia, Canada, B2Z 1P8
To order, phone 1-800-NIMBUS9
(1-800-646-2879)

Printed in Canada

THE CANADA COUNCIL | LE CONSEIL DES ARTS
FOR THE ARTS | DU CANADA
SINCE 1957 | DEPUIS 1957

Dedication

This book is dedicated to my good friends,
the Nyajeka family:
Shingai, Margaret, Tandiwe, and Shingai Jr.

Acknowledgements

I would like to thank the following people for their help in making
this book possible:

George Elliott Clarke, for opening the door;

Sam Bufalini and Doug MacKay, for letting me in;

Shane Ross, for keeping my space;

Dale Farmer-Saunders and her family, for their support;

Michele Raymond, for inspiring the book's title.

Contents

On Charles Saunders, or The artist as journalist

I first met Charles R. Saunders shortly after he had made the risky decision to quit Ottawa and relocate himself — typewriter, manuscripts, and screenplay contracts — to Halifax. It was, as I recall, a bright day in early August, 1985, when I walked into Percy Paris' Gottingen Street storefront office of *The Jet Journal*, his proud but struggling black provincial newspaper, and was introduced to Charles, a brother writer. I'll never forget that meeting. Though Charles had already published three celebrated fantasy novels in New York City, he had no time for airs. This big, big-hearted, big-laughing, and bushy-afro'd man was gracious, erudite, and witty — the quintessence of bonhomie. Charles was, then, an instant inspiration. Here was a black man, just like me, but also a published author with an international audience, a self-exiled Pennsylvanian and ex-Upper Canadian, who saw in Black Nova Scotia a community — no, a people — shamefully rich in — yes, music and athletics, but also politics, theology, literature, history, *drama*. Thanks to Charles' fresh and refreshing vision, I began to see Black Nova Scotia — or, rather, Africadia — with new, lovingly curious, and deeply appreciative eyes. He helped me to adore the poetry in our speech and the philosophical purpose in our struggle.

Charlie Saunders' gift to all Nova Scotia has been, I think, to help us see ourselves with truer clarity. In his columns, we're not just marginals dwelling in some foggy Ultima Thule, but a uniquely motley clutch of peoples facing the same issues that bedevil most of humanity, striking our own artistic stances and finding our own socio-political answers in a grand, peninsular theatre, on a proscenium stage thrust into the Atlantic. Anyone who wants to understand Nova Scotians at the end of the second millennium can do no better than read Saunders' commentaries.

A scrupulous publicly-minded and sensitive columnist, Saunders has canvassed every problem and accomplishment in what is euphemistically called "race relations," especially of the black-white variety, that has unfolded in Nova Scotia over the past decade. Of course, given that Nova Scotia was once a slave society (just like Mississippi) and later allowed only segregated educational and employment prospects (just like Alabama), there have been plenty of racial *contretemps* to address, even though the public display of prejudice is now considered very bad form.

Charles' interest in these matters was demonstrated soon after his move to Halifax in the spring of 1985. Though he'd always known of the existence of the indigenous blacks of Nova Scotia, it was only after visiting Halifax for the first time, during a sci-fi convention early that year, that he decided to make the city his home. Black Haligonians reminded him of his family and friends back in Pennsylvania, and their down-to-earth accent, down-home cuisine, and down-to-soul gospel were uplifting and upstanding. Nevertheless, he sure chose a fine time to relocate. That summer African-Nova Scotians — or Africadians — were questioning the prosecution of two recent killings that seemed to showcase, once again, a for-whites-only justice system. In the first instance, Deborah Wright's white murderer received a sentence for manslaughter that seems disturbingly lenient, given that he'd stabbed her 11 times and left her to bleed to death in a gutter on a frozen Halifax street. The second case involved Graham Cromwell, a Weymouth Falls man, whose white killer was acquitted of manslaughter charges by an all-white jury that the killer's own lawyer branded as "red-neck."

Though new to Nova Scotia, Saunders was not new to these issues. As an African-American who'd resisted Nixon's Vietnam War by escaping to Canada (just in time to experience the October Crisis), he had witnessed terroristic police actions on many fronts. Sharing the Africadian community's rage at the "Just Us" system, Saunders supported the protests that welled up round the Wright and Cromwell cases, and he scribed pointed analyses for *The Jet Journal* and later *The Rap*. Following a centuries-old, African-North American tradition, then, Charles came to perform journalism as a *protest*-oriented, *engagé* art.

Still, Charles' work is not merely an oppositional practice, just as Africadia is not only a site of anger. Since 1983, the descendants of Black Loyalists and Black Refugees have been advancing their own Cultural Renaissance — in every art and in many professions. Charles' articles, histories, and fiction have been central to this epochal movement. If one of the most vital aspects of the Africadian Cultural Renaissance was the founding of the Africville Genealogical Society in 1983, one of the society's most distinguished acts was to commission Saunders to author "A Visit to Africville," a superb, New Journalist recreation of the textures and personalities of the now-demolished Africadian village. First published in 1989, Saunders' beloved piece has been reprinted many times. It has made Africville a "virtual" community for the many thousands who never had a chance to see or visit it before its destruction — in a spasm of reckless "social engineering" — in 1970. Saunders has further contributed to the Africadian Cultural Renaissance by authoring lauded histories of Africadian boxers and the Nova Scotia Home for Colored Children, as well as by writing a CBC-broadcast radio drama about the life of Sam Langford, one of Africadia's greatest pugilists.

But it's his work as an eclectic and encyclopedic columnist for *The Daily News* of Halifax that has made Saunders the public symbol of the Africadian Cultural Renaissance. Strangely — but happily — he inherited this career from me. Indeed, from October 1988 to February 1989, I wrote a black-focused, public-affairs column for *The Daily News*, by faxing down copy from Ottawa, where I was living at the time, having, in a sense, exchanged cities with Saunders. When I bowed out I suggested one more exchange, namely, that the paper ask Saunders to take over the column. It did so, and Halifax and Nova Scotia have not been the same since. Hallelujah and all praise to Saunders for his meditative art — and for all the beautiful changes.

George Elliott Clarke
Department of English
Duke University
Durham, North Carolina
December 1998

Come-from-away

More than 200 years ago, blacks in Britain's 13 rebellious North American colonies were offered a choice between continued slavery and a chance for freedom. Those who chose freedom were resettled in Nova Scotia, one of the colonies that did not join the ultimately successful revolution.

A generation later, during the War of 1812, freedom was again offered to American slaves who made their way behind British lines. And, again, the majority of those who accepted that offer came to Nova Scotia.

The people involved in those two migrations of hope, along with those who were held in slavery in Nova Scotia, formed the basis of a unique black community: one that is small in numbers, but looms in significance; one that contains the largest indigenous black population in Canada   the Prestons — as well as the most iconic and symbolic of places — Africville. African-Nova Scotians such as boxers George Dixon and Sam Langford, war hero William Hall, and singer Portia White, have made their mark not only in the province, but also throughout Canada and the world.

Yet Nova Scotia's black community remains — like those elsewhere in North America — both hopeful and beleaguered; racking up "firsts" that all too often become "onlys;" taking the proverbial two steps forward and one step back; wondering when racism will finally be eradicated, or, at the very least, rendered as irrelevant and absurd as the Flat Earth theory.

I've often wondered what my choice would have been had I lived in slavery in the U.S. 200 years ago. Would I have taken my chances with the revolutionaries, with their Declaration of Independence that was written by slaveowners? Or would I have trusted the British, the ones who brought slavery to their colonies in the first place?

Of course, that question cannot be answered. But I think there's a strong possibility I would have gambled that the British would honor their promise of freedom, and I would have been among the 3,000 Black Loyalists who stepped off ships in Halifax in 1783. Had one of my ancestors made such a choice, I would have been born a Nova Scotian rather than a Pennsylvanian.

But my forebears elected to stay in what would eventually become the United States. That's why I am an African Nova Scotian by choice rather than birth. I arrived here in the summer of 1985 and, while there have been ups and downs since then, I have never regretted my decision to live here.

Still, I realize I will always be a come-from-away, the term Nova Scotians and other Maritimers use to describe those who don't have a long family history in these parts. I have found, though, that one can be a come-from-away but still find a home in this land by the sea.

In this world of high mobility, people have two homes: the one they were born in, and the one they make. Years ago, those two homes were more often than not one and the same. Now, more often than not, homes are made in distant places, and come-from-aways are commonplace rather than curiosities.

I have made my home in Nova Scotia. And I want my home to be the best place it can possibly be. That is why I write my columns of commentary on African Nova Scotians' aspirations and accomplishments, problems and pitfalls, dreams and reality. And that is why I have collected them in this book. By doing so, I hope to give back at least a fraction of what the black community of Nova Scotia has given to me.

Charles Saunders
November 1998

School days

The Cole Harbour High fights of 1989

In January 1989, several months before I began to write my columns, racially motivated brawls broke out over a three-day period at Cole Harbour District High School. A video clip of two youths trading punches — one black, the other white — played repeatedly over local and national airwaves.

Eighteen people, 10 black and eight white, faced assault charges and entered into a provincial justice system that had a year earlier been pilloried because of its mishandling of the Donald Marshall case, in which a 17-year-old Cape Breton Island Mi'kmaq had been wrongfully convicted of killing a black youth.

The fights triggered a flurry of bureaucratic action. By the middle of 1989, plans were under way to build a second high school in the area to alleviate the overcrowding thought to have been an underlying cause of the violence.

However, the notion of a new school worried some black parents who sent their children to Cole Harbour High because they considered such a move a retreat from the ideal of school integration.

Black parents are outnumbered at a public meeting about the racial brawls at Cole Harbour District High School. *(Paul Darrow/The Daily News)*

Integration is more than merely moving students
June 11, 1989

Hot on the heels of the controversy surrounding the schoolyard fights at Cole Harbour High School comes the debate concerning the location of a new secondary school in the Cole Harbour/Prestons/Eastern Passage/Colby Village area. Racial integration in the school system is one of the focal points of that debate.

Those who oppose the proposed Caldwell Road site for the new school say that such a location would have a negative effect on efforts to integrate black students from the Prestons into the school population. In response, some of those who favor Caldwell Road are saying: "Who cares?"

A more appropriate question might be: "What do we mean by 'integration'?"

"Integration" has meant different things at different times. In the 1950s and '60s, it meant "access." Civil rights activists in Canada and the United States used a variety of tactics to fight for access to services and institutions denied to blacks through law and custom. Employment, housing, and education were the major targets for the "integration as access" movement. There were minor targets as well, such as lunch counters, waiting rooms, and barber shops. Once blacks gained equal access to these institutions and services, a state of "integration" was declared.

The schools were a different matter. Until the mid-1950s, racially segregated schools existed on both sides of the Canada-U.S. border. By no means did all black children attend black-only schools. In southern states and some parts of Nova Scotia, though, a large proportion of black students were educated in segregated schools.

Advocates of school segregation pointed to the principle of "separate but equal," meaning that separation of black and white students was fine as long as both races had equal facilities. But the facilities were far from equal. Black schools routinely received only a fraction of the financial support granted to white schools. Teachers were underpaid and under-qualified. Books and equipment were substandard. Despite heroic efforts made by dedicated teachers and principals in such schools, the education

15

they provided was separate and unequal. Their graduates were not equipped to compete in the world beyond the segregated classroom.

To the civil rights leaders of the 1950s, the answer to the black education problem was not to pour more money into the segregated system in order to "equalize" black and white schools. The principle they drove home in the courts and legislatures was this: "Separate is by definition unequal."

In other words, even if the teachers at black and white schools had the same qualifications, the libraries had the same number of books, and the swimming pools held the same amount of water, the fact of segregation in itself created a situation of inequality.

Policies based on the principle that "separate is unequal" led to the legal abolition of racially segregated schools. Subsequent policies once again amounted to a question of access.

Under the umbrella of "integration," black and white students were to gain equal access to educational facilities — and each other.

Unfortunately, the realities of school integration have not always matched these ideals. Too often, "integration" has come to mean "movement of bodies" at one extreme and "forced assimilation" at the other. The ideals that provided the initial motivation for "integration" are sometimes buried beneath a mountain of pass/fail percentages and other statistics. Today, the concept of "integration" is synonymous with raised voices, clenched fists, and angry petitions.

But it doesn't have to be that way. Let's remove the quotation marks from "integration" and attempt to understand what it really means. It means more than simply using buses to transplant black students from one school to another.

True educational integration works at three levels: students, staff, and curriculum. In most cases, the process has worked only on the student level. On the level of teachers and staff, the record has been poor. On the curriculum level, progress has been almost non-existent.

Black and other minority teachers fulfill the requirements of true integration in two ways. First and foremost, they provide positive role models for minority students. Of course, they can also serve the same purpose for white students.

Second, minority teachers, administrative staff, and guidance counsellors provide an image and an example that can serve to counteract negative racial stereotypes. This can be of special benefit to white students who have absorbed such stereotypes from parents and peers.

If the student body of a school is integrated, but not the teaching staff, then the job of integration is less than half-done. But if the curriculum isn't integrated, then the school system rests on faulty foundations.

A curriculum that fails to take into account the current and historical contributions of blacks and other minorities to all aspects of human development and progress is a segregated curriculum. An integrated school that teaches a segregated curriculum is a contradiction in terms.

Over the past 30 years, the school system and the society that surrounds it have come a long way from the "separate but equal" doctrine. But we have not yet reached the goal of fully integrating the schools on all educational levels.

As the Cole Harbour debate indicates, "integration" is still seen as a matter of moving bodies from one place to another. And that's not what the visionaries of the 1950s had in mind when they spoke out against segregated schools.

A new high school was built at Auburn Drive, not far from the location of Cole Harbour High School. Black students from East Preston were assigned to the new school; students from North Preston continued to attend Cole Harbour High. Both schools remained integrated — at the student level, at least. In the mean time, the quest for change and justice continued.

Cole Harbour aftermath offers hope
August 31, 1989

Twenty years from now, historians may well view 1989 as a pivotal year in the course of race relations in Nova Scotia. 1989 began with an incident of racial violence at Cole Harbour District High School. The incident involved black students from the Preston area and white students from Eastern Passage. Non-students from both the black and white communities were involved as well. National headlines and an impassioned public debate continued well after the situation at the school subsided.

The end of 1989 may see significant progress toward changes that are long overdue. The events that followed the fighting and the subsequent laying of charges by the RCMP have led to an unprecedented opportunity to offset the effects of nearly three centuries of injustice.

Will Nova Scotians take advantage of this opportunity? Or will the systemic racism that has marred the history of the 18th, 19th, and 20th centuries in this province continue well into the 21st?

One group that has seized the opportunity is the Parent-Student Association of Preston (PSAP). Formed during the turmoil following the incident, PSAP is in the midst of a battle to change the conditions Preston-area students encounter in the education system. The battle is being fought on two fronts: the Halifax County-Bedford District School Board and the Attorney General's office. On both fronts, the PSAP has faced strong resistance.

For several months, both the PSAP and the Eastern Passage Parents' Group have been pressuring Attorney General Tom McInnis to call an inquiry into the problem of racism and discrimination in the provincial educational system. McInnis has steadfastly refused to consider such an inquiry on the grounds that the school board has set up four committees on "cross-cultural understanding" to deal with the situation.

In a July 12 community meeting that was closed to the media at the attorney general's request, McInnis suggested that the PSAP work with the school board and its committees rather than press for an inquiry.

But the school board has refused to grant the PSAP status on the committees. One board member said he didn't see what "positive result" a proposed meeting with the PSAP might have had. Adding insult to injury, another board member went so far as to express "concern" over PSAP participation because some of the Preston parents' children were facing charges stemming from the January violence.

In other words, committees that were intended to promote "understanding" are slamming the door in the faces of the people they're allegedly attempting to understand.

Had the board been willing to receive the PSAP's input when it was offered, it would have learned that the Preston area parents question the committees' emphasis on "cross-cultural understanding."

According to PSAP president Evangeline Cain-Grant, the committees' focus is inappropriate. "The model they're using deals with the problems of recent immigrants," says Cain-Grant. "We are not recent immigrants. We've been here more than 200 years. Our problem isn't 'cross-cultural understanding.' It's racism."

The committees' final recommendations have not yet been released. Once they are, the PSAP is certain to reject them on the above grounds and continue to call for an inquiry. What will the Attorney General and the School Board say then?

The PSAP's second battlefront is far more complex. Of 18 people (10 blacks and eight whites) originally charged by the RCMP in connection with the January incident, five (all black) still face criminal charges. The others have either been acquitted or had their charges dropped.

In McInnis' view, the fact that only blacks still face charges is a "coincidence." But the PSAP doesn't buy that explanation.

Through Halifax lawyer Davies Bagambiire, the five defendants have filed a lawsuit against the Attorney General's office in the Supreme Court of Nova Scotia. The defendants claim that the charges against them are in violation of the Canadian Charter of Rights and Freedoms. The suit contends that the RCMP's investigation leading to the laying of charges was "racially discriminatory."

Reflecting the opinion of the defendants' families as well as that of many who are not directly involved in the case, the suit alleges that the RCMP based its charges on biased evidence collected from white witnesses. Black witnesses were either ignored or arrested. Therefore, according to Bagambiire's statement of claim, the remaining charges should be dismissed.

It should be noted that the PSAP believes no one — black or white — should have been charged in the incident. Many whites share this view.

The Attorney General has responded by asking the Supreme Court to dismiss Bagambiire's lawsuit. Whatever its outcome, this legal action promises to be the most notable — and embarrassing — proceeding in this province since the Donald Marshall inquiry.

Eight months after the Cole Harbour incident, there are still skeptics who attempt to belittle its importance, saying it was nothing more than a "snowball fight" magnified by the media. Within a broader historical context, however, such a viewpoint is extremely narrow-minded. The race problems at Cole Harbour High did not start with a snowball thrown on January 9, 1989.

In reality, the stage for the confrontation was set nearly three centuries ago. The prejudice and inequality that marked the beginnings of black-white coexistence in Nova Scotia molded the attitudes of future generations on both sides.

Over the years, white attitudes toward blacks have ranged from paternalistic tolerance to open contempt and hostility. Black attitudes toward whites have ranged from envy and awe to bitterness and hatred. Yet among both groups, genuine respect and understanding have sometimes developed despite the odds.

The co-operation between parents from the Preston area and Eastern Passage indicates that a common cause can transcend long-standing differences. That co-operation began shortly after the incident, when tension between the two groups was at its highest. Instead of adding fuel to the racial fire, parents in the Prestons and Eastern Passage set an example by working together. Their actions and words provided a lesson that was not lost on the students of Cole Harbour High.

And therein lies the hope that this time, real change could be approaching in the near future.

Back to school at Cole Harbour High
September 3, 1989

You're 17 years old.

You're a student at Cole Harbour District High School.

You're black.

You're from North Preston.

School starts next week.

You know your school was the centre of nationwide publicity because of a series of fights earlier this year. Some say the incident was blown out of proportion. You know it was just the tip of an iceberg that's more than 200 years old. You didn't want any trouble. But when it came, you stood up for yourself.

You're not sorry you did.

You know most of your teachers try to be fair. But there are also some who think they know everything about you just from what you look like or where you live. You hope you don't get any teachers like that this year.

You get along fine with most of the other students. But you know there are some who need to look down on you so they can feel better about themselves. These are the ones who do the name-calling, snowball-throwing, and fist-fighting. If you strike back, there's a good chance you'll get the blame, whether you started it or not. You might even get charged by the RCMP, or hounded through the courts by the Attorney General's office. You try to keep your anger locked up inside you. But sometimes you get pushed too far and too hard.

Your parents are fighting for an inquiry into racism in the school system. You're glad they're doing it, and you give them all the help you can. You hear the Attorney General say there's no need for an inquiry because the school board has set up a committee to look into the matter. He says your parents should work with the committee. A week earlier, that committee told your parents to get lost. You feel bitter and confused.

When your parents speak out against injustice, they are accused of "fanning the flames of discrimination." But you know who started the fire.

You listen to the debates on where a second high school in your district should be built. You know there are some parents who have no problems as far as their children going to school with you is concerned. But there are others who want the new school built as far away from you as possible. You ask yourself why they feel that way. You know there's nothing wrong with you. But sometimes you catch yourself wondering.

You know the situation at your school isn't simply a matter of black and white. There are white parents standing alongside your own because their children get pigeonholed the same way you do. You wonder why some people are so afraid of this alliance.

You wonder why the people who have 99.9 per cent of the money and power don't want you to have even your little 0.1 per cent, and will do anything they can to prevent you from increasing your share.

You're from North Preston.

School starts next week.

You're prepared for the worst.

But you're hoping for the best.

Black students pay price of inaction
December 3, 1989

Public inquiries of all kinds have recently monopolized headlines in Canada. The Donald Marshall Inquiry in Nova Scotia, the Native Justice Inquiry in Manitoba, the Air Safety Inquiry in Ontario, the Mount Cashel Inquiry in Newfoundland — all these proceedings have lifted the rugs under which racism, discrimination, negligence, incompetence, and even brutal sex abuse have been swept.

Is it any wonder the very word "inquiry" has become anathema to many politicians? The situation is reminiscent of a Raid commercial. You've seen them a thousand times. A bunch of nasty-looking bugs is having a good time chewing up the breadcrumbs. Then suddenly a giant can of Raid appears. The terrified insects scream, "RAID! AAAAAAA!" Moments later, they perish in a cloud of insecticide. These days, if you mention the word "inquiry" to a politician, you get a similar reaction: "INQUIRY! AAAAAAA!"

Case in point: ever since the Cole Harbour High School incident last January, the Parent-Student Association of Preston has been calling for an inquiry into racism in the Nova Scotia education system. But the provincial government continues to deny the need for such an investigation.

Last summer, Attorney-General Tom McInnis told the PSAP there was no point in even considering an inquiry before the Halifax County-Bedford District School Board had completed its own investigation of the matter. "Work with the school board," McInnis assured concerned parents. "Give them a chance."

The PSAP was calling for a province-wide inquiry, not one limited to Halifax County schools. The Cole Harbour High incident and its aftermath were indicative of a larger problem beyond the scope of one school board's jurisdiction.

At any rate, not long after McInnis's statement, the Halifax County board refused to allow the PSAP representation on the "cross-cultural understanding committee" that was supposed to be dealing with the problems of Preston-area students. And recently, the board was unable to agree on the adoption of a simple statement committing itself to "anti-racist education." This impasse came after the board had sent a representative to a Toronto conference on that very topic.

Some "chance," eh?

Based on the school board's performance to date, it shouldn't be difficult to understand why PSAP and its supporters are continuing to press for an inquiry.

Yet the government continues to resist. At a recent conference on the lessons of the Africville relocation of the 1960s, Education Minister Ron Giffin said an inquiry isn't necessary because he already knows there's racism in the system. Giffin argues there's no need to spend taxpayers' money to belabor an obvious point. But the purpose of the proposed inquiry isn't to "prove" or "disprove" the existence of racism in the education system. Nor is the purpose to nail anyone to the wall, or drag anyone's reputation through the mud, or make continuous headlines on the six o'clock news.

And the PSAP certainly isn't calling for an inquiry because it's "fashionable" to do so, as Attorney-General McInnis once implied. For all the publicity other inquiries have generated, the matters they've investigated have been deadly serious, not "fashionable."

In general, the purpose of an inquiry is to uncover the answer to a central question. The central question of the Marshall Inquiry was: "Why did Donald Marshall spend 11 years in prison for a crime he didn't commit?"

The central question for an inquiry on racism in education should be: "In what way can the educational system best meet the needs of students of all races, colors, nationalities, and linguistic backgrounds?"

The high illiteracy rate in this country indicates that the system works in a haphazard way even for white students. But minority students face additional obstacles. Most black students who succeed in school do so despite the system. Most black students who fail do so because of the system.

When any child enters kindergarten, he or she is embarking on a gamble that will last 12 years (or less). A look at dropout rates and achievement levels reveals that in this gamble, the deck is stacked against black children. A thorough and constructive examination of the system would help to even the odds.

As PSAP President Evangeline Cain-Grant puts it, "We're tired of putting our children in a system that plays Russian Roulette with their education. An inquiry would be the best way to develop specific solutions to the problems black students face in the schools."

There are only 10 years left in this century. Will it take that long to remove the residue of institutional racism from our educational system so that black and other minority children have the same chance to succeed as any other children?

By the middle of 1990, the cases of the Cole Harbour High brawlers that had not already been disposed of through the dropping of charges reached trial. Two young black men were convicted of "causing a disturbance." But the conduct of the trial of another defendant bordered on the farcical .

The verdict:
Something's wrong here
July 15, 1990

Something's wrong here ...
Eighteen months after the racial fights at Cole Harbour District High School, three young black men were found guilty of "causing a disturbance" in connection with the incident.

Out of 18 people originally charged — 10 blacks and eight whites — only Steven Fraser, John Thompson, and Marvin Smith were convicted. Later, in a miscue that would have embarrassed even a kangaroo court, Fraser's conviction was cancelled because he had never been charged with the offense for which he was on trial.

Another black youth, Deon Provo, still faces trial on charges stemming from the incident.

Something's wrong here ...
In handing down her verdict, provincial court judge Fran Potts made a significant comment: "It's unfortunate that many others — equally or more guilty — were not successfully prosecuted ...." This is the same judge who had earlier ruled that the RCMP's investigation of the brawls was "flawed, but not racially biased."

So Judge Potts went ahead and convicted the three North Preston defendants on the basis of an investigation she considers "flawed." She convicted them while acknowledging that they were not the only guilty parties. But if the investigation was "flawed," why weren't all the charges summarily dismissed? Why were these three blacks the only ones to be penalized for a *mêlée* involving dozens of participants of both races?

Something's wrong here ....

Crown Prosecutor Bob McCarroll said: "The argument that you shouldn't convict because the underlying tone is racial doesn't mean a hill of beans."

But race was not an "underlying tone" in the fights at Cole Harbour High. It was the only tone. Even Judge Potts agreed that racism was a primary factor in the brawls.

The white non-students who occupied school grounds did not do so because they didn't like the color of the black students' jackets. (It's true that some of the blacks involved in the fighting were also non-students. But there's reason to believe that the blacks came to the school in response to rumors of an "invasion.")

The motivation for the physical and verbal assaults on blacks at the school was race prejudice, pure and simple. If it wasn't racial, why were the black students called "niggers"?

Does McCarroll think "nigger" is some mild epithet, like "nerd" or "goofball," with no racial connotation? Does he think that when a white calls a black a "nigger," it has nothing to do with race?

The long history of racial tension between the Prestons and Eastern Passage amounts to a lot more than a "hill of beans." But then McCarroll has some "beans" of his own to contend with.

It was McCarroll who assured defence lawyer Davies Bagambiire that Steven Fraser was indeed charged with "causing a disturbance" even though Fraser's name was not on the court information sheet.

Something's wrong here ....

Throughout the year and a half that's passed since the incident, a particular clip of video footage has been used over and over on local and national news programs. It shows a black youth in a denim jacket throwing three punches at a white youth in a checkered shirt. The camera angle gives the impression that the black youth is beating up the white one, primarily because you can't see what the white kid is doing. From a different angle, you might have seen some punches thrown by the white youth. And a different clip might have caught other whites in belligerent acts.

This clip sets the tone of public perception of the incident. It's as though a bunch of Mike Tysons and Buster Douglases plowed through the schoolyard, beating the crap out of some innocent little Doogie Howsers. Intentional or unintentional, the message of the clip is: it's the blacks' fault. The old stereotype of young black males as generic troublemakers is reinforced.

Something's wrong here ....

The prosecution has said that charges against white defendants were dropped due to "lack of evidence." The evidence against Fraser, Thompson, and Smith consisted of eyewitness testimony. In other words, the prosecution was able to find witnesses willing to testify that they saw the three black defendants throwing punches and kicks during the brawl. Why wasn't the Attorney General's office or the RCMP able to locate anyone willing to testify that they saw whites throwing punches or kicks at blacks?

Defence witnesses testified that whites followed blacks through the halls of the school taunting them and challenging them to fight. Why didn't the RCMP use the testimony of these witnesses to develop cases against potential white suspects? Or did the RCMP investigators simply tune out any statements that implicated whites in "causing the disturbance"?

Something's wrong here ...

It could have been worse. Much worse. The black youths could have been charged with assault rather than causing a disturbance. They could have been sentenced to jail terms instead of the probation and conditional discharge Judge Potts handed down. The relatively light sentences seem to indicate that the judge is aware of a disparity between the letter and the spirit of the law in this case.

Judge Potts appears to be saying she can only pass judgement on the cases that are put in front of her, and it's not her fault most of the guilty parties slipped through some convenient cracks in the system. But how relevant is that reasoning when one of the defendants in front of her isn't even properly charged with an offence?

But that's cold comfort to two young black men who were trying to defend themselves against attackers who outnumbered them. It's cold comfort to Steven Fraser, who experienced a *Twilight Zone* trial on a phantom charge.

Neither Judge Potts nor anyone else can adequately explain to Marvin Smith and John Thompson why they are going to have convictions on their records while the whites who were harassing them got off scot-free.

Something's wrong here ...

Media reports have described the black community's reaction to the convictions as "anger" and "outrage." Some may perceive that anger as prejudice against whites. That perception misses the point. Imagine what would have happened if charges against all the black defendants in the Cole Harbour case had been dropped, with whites the only ones ultimately convicted. All hell would have broken loose in the white community.

It's not over yet. Deon Provo will have his day in court this November. And the convictions of Thompson and Smith will be appealed. Perhaps then the three youths will find out why theirs were the only cases that were "successfully prosecuted."

Until then, blacks in the Preston area continue to wonder: Is this justice or just us?

Fraser deserves apology, compensation
July 22, 1990

The confrontation between the Mohawks and the police at Oka, Quebec is not the only racially influenced standoff in Canada today. There are several standoffs going on right here in Nova Scotia. The most recent has been the case of Steven Fraser, a young black man from North Preston, who was convicted on an offence for which he had not been charged.

Although Fraser's conviction was nullified once the error was discovered, his family still asked the province for an apology, plus compensation for their legal costs. These requests were reasonable. The Frasers weren't asking for the moon. They were only asking that the justice system do right by their son.

Unfortunately, Attorney General Tom McInnis doesn't see it that way. By his lights, neither an apology nor compensation is in order. As far as he's concerned, Fraser was "convicted on evidence properly presented." McInnis dismisses the fact that Fraser was not "properly" charged as a mere "technical error."

What McInnis fails to explain is how evidence can be "properly presented" in a case that should never have gone to trial in the first place.

Fingers can be pointed and excuses can be trotted out until the cows come home. But the fact remains that Fraser sat through a trial and heard a judge pronounce him guilty on a charge that wasn't even entered on the court information sheet. The Attorney General's Department only adds to its own embarrassment by refusing to say: "We're sorry."

McInnis appears to be suffering from a case of selective sympathy. When the results of the Donald Marshall inquiry were announced, the Attorney General was overflowing with the milk of human kindness. He accepted every one of the inquiry's criticisms of the province's justice system. He even had dinner with Marshall's parents.

But for the blacks in the Preston area, that milk dried up three years ago, when a new sewer system was installed there. If you talk to him about the current unrest in the black community, he'll spread his hands and say, "Why are these people kicking me after all I've done for them?"

To which the community can only respond: "We're not kicking you. You're kicking us."

Because only blacks were convicted in the legal aftermath of the Cole Harbour High brawls, and because the Attorney General continues to deny repeated calls for an inquiry into the problem of racism in the education system, a group of Preston area residents and others are embarking on a public fast. Perhaps the growls from the stomachs of the demonstrators will send McInnis a message words have thus far failed to convey.

A stand against hate in the heart of Halifax
July 29, 1990

It started in the rain — a Monday morning Maritimes downpour. The rain drummed steadily against the blue tarpaulin sheet that was the only shelter for a group of people determined to bring public attention to the problem of racism in Nova Scotia. The tarp and the protesters were located at the Grand Parade, in the heart of Halifax.

Most of the protesters were black. But there were whites involved as well. You don't have to be black to be aware of the effects of racism.

Over the past few years, the Grand Parade has been the site of protests that span the political spectrum. This week, it was the turn of the Parent-Student Association of Preston to vent its frustration against a provincial government that seems to need a hearing aid whenever racial grievances are mentioned.

For seven days, the protesters took turns fasting for rotating 24-hour periods. Neither rain nor the heat of the summer sun deterred the fasters from their purpose. Even City Hall's puzzling refusal to allow them to spend their nights at the Grand Parade failed to turn them around.

The purpose of the fast was twofold. First, it was a protest against the recent convictions of two young black men on charges arising from the January 1989 fights at Cole Harbour High School. Second, it represented a continuation of a long-standing demand for a public inquiry into racism in the Nova Scotia education system — a demand repeatedly rejected by provincial cabinet minsters.

The latest nay-sayer was Education Minister Ron Giffin.

Giffin recently said a full-scale inquiry on racism isn't necessary because a committee is now looking into the matter, and its recommendations are due before long.

But PSAP and its supporters argue that the problem is beyond the scope of Giffin's committee. A full-scale inquiry would possess the capacity to identify and seek solutions to the factors that led to racial strife at Cole Harbour High and other educational institutions. As well, the persistence of high dropout rates among black students and the practice of "streaming" blacks and Mi'kmaq into dead-end courses would come under investigation.

One thing the inquiry would not be is a witch-hunt. Its purpose would not be to seek out and punish racist individuals within the system. Its purpose would be to find ways to restructure the system so that Nova Scotians of all colors could enjoy equal educational opportunities.

The fast was an attempt to alert the government to the depth of disquiet about racism in both the black and the white communities. If prayer and fasting cannot open closed eyes and unplug clogged ears — what can? That's the question PSAP and its supporters will be asking each other if the government continues to dismiss their concerns.

The fast ended uneventfully. Steven Fraser received neither compensation nor an apology. And no inquiry into the Cole Harbour High fights was ever called. But the aftermath of the event did not go away . . .

Cole Harbour fallout continues
November 26, 1990

Nearly two years have passed since the racial fights at Cole Harbour District High School. But the fallout from that incident continues. Last week, Deon Provo, a 20-year-old from North Preston, was acquitted on weapons charges. An MITV cameraman had videotaped Provo carrying *nunchaku* sticks, an Oriental martial arts device popularized in the West by Bruce Lee movies. The tape was shown over and over again across Canada.

However, Judge Felix Cacchione ruled that Crown Attorney Bob McCarroll had not proven that Provo intended to use the sticks to cause "death, injury, threats, or intimidation." His implication is that Provo was guilty only of being caught in the media spotlight.

North Preston is probably breathing a sigh of relief over Provo's acquittal. But the prosecution is considering an appeal of Judge Cacchione's verdict. The expense involved in fighting such an appeal would further erode the community's finances.

The judicial scorecard in the Cole Harbour High incident now stands as follows:

Eighteen young men, 10 black and eight white, were charged after the brawls.

All eight whites and six of the blacks were either acquitted or had their cases dismissed. Four blacks were brought to trial.

Three (Marvin Smith, John Thompson, and Steven Fraser) were found guilty by Judge Fran Potts on a charge of "causing a disturbance."

Of those three, Fraser had his conviction dismissed because he had not been formally charged with the offence.

One (Provo) was acquitted.

Although Provo's case was the last one brought to court, the legal battles aren't over. Judge Potts's convictions of Smith and Thompson are under appeal. And the Crown may appeal Provo's acquittal.

As well, Fraser's family sought an apology and compensation for his erroneous conviction. Then Attorney General Tom McInnis snubbed that request, saying the matter was just a "clerical error." Well, one person's clerical error is another's travesty of justice. Perhaps the new attorney general will approach the matter differently.

The appeal process may drag on well into next year. It appears that the consequences of three days of televised violence have proven very far-reaching indeed.

Not all the fallout from the Cole Harbour incident has been negative. During the same week Provo was on trial, the school hosted a human-rights conference. The conference was one of many efforts Cole Harbour High has made to defuse racial tensions. Others include a black literature course taught by poet Maxine Tynes, and an expansion of Black History Week. Beyond Cole Harbour High, committees have been formed on race relations as well as the "education of black learners."

Despite these efforts, there have still been repeated calls for an inquiry into racism in the education system. Those calls have been summarily spurned by the provincial education and attorney general's departments. "Unnecessary" is the operative word in these rejections.

However, the Halifax County-Bedford school board has hired a full-time race-relations director, Janis Jones-Darrell. To be more specific, Jones-Darrell is in charge of race relations, cross-cultural understanding, and human rights.

Jones-Darrell has already held race-relations seminars for teachers and school officials. She has also proposed an anti-racism policy that has been accepted in principle by the board.

These efforts are all commendable. Still, they seem to be aimed primarily at promoting an atmosphere of racial harmony that will preclude any repetition of the fights that rocked the province.

There's nothing wrong with that goal. But there still needs to be a long, hard look at the conditions that cause so many black students to perceive the education system as nothing more than a long and frustrating obstacle course.

In July 1993, the Nova Scotia Court of Appeal upheld the convictions of Marvin Smith and John Thompson. By the mid-1990s, it was believed by most that racial violence at Cole Harbour High had run its course.

North Preston residents protest the siting of a proposed landfill near their community. *(Stu Ducklow/The Daily News)*

Not in my black yard

The battle against the East Lake landfill

During the early 1990s, metro Halifax, which included the municipalities of Halifax, Dartmouth, Bedford, and Halifax County, faced the unenviable task of deciding the location of a new landfill site. The old landfill, which opened in 1977 in Sackville, was scheduled to close in 1993.

The Metro Authority, which represented the four governments before they merged to become the Halifax Regional Municipality in 1995, developed a long list of possible sites. Some of those sites were located near black communities. Objections arose immediately.

Landfill fight:
Preston exercises its new clout
September 15, 1991

The Metropolitan Authority's recent decision to eliminate a site near the Preston area as a potential location for a landfill is welcome news. Ratepayers' associations from both North and East Preston had objected vehemently to a report that included two sites, East Lake and Woody Lake, located near their communities.

Woody Lake has now been crossed off the list because it isn't large enough to meet site-selection criteria. East Lake remains under consideration.

However, 10 years ago, both areas were identified as watershed and therefore unsuitable for landfill. The report that ruled the lakes out then was prepared by the same consulting firm that included them on a revised list the Metropolitan Authority received last month. The perceived flip-flop sparked anger in the area.

At first glance, this incident appears to be just another example of the "not in my back yard" syndrome. The Prestons weren't the only community in Halifax County to discourage any notion of dumping garbage in their vicinity. Residents of Head of St. Margaret's Bay are protesting just as vigorously.

But the predominantly black Preston area has an additional motivation to object. In a news release issued after the announcement of the updated list, the ratepayer's associations and District 8 County Councillor Wayne Adams referred to the location of a garbage dump at Africville, a Halifax black community that was razed during the 1960s.

Africville residents didn't want the dump in their area when it was proposed in the preceding decade. But they got it, whether they liked it or not. The community did not possess enough political clout to keep the unwanted facility away.

Eventually, the dump became identified with the community, and the community with the dump. Within a few years, Africville was referred to as the "community built around the dump," when in fact the community predated the facility by more than a century. This perception influenced the ultimate decision to bulldoze Africville.

Forty years ago, the people of Africville couldn't say "Not in my back yard." Today, the people of the Preston area can.

The winnowing process continued. Later in 1991, three sites were chosen as "finalists" for the new dump site. One of them was East Lake.

Hidden road to freedom
December 29, 1991

The recent designation of a site near the Preston area as one of the three finalists for the location of a new landfill in Halifax County has caused heated debate. Although the historical value of the site, known as East Lake, has been dismissed by some, Preston residents and the Black Cultural Centre have indicated it may be the location of the first black Preston settlement. The basis for such speculation is the presence of foundations, unmarked graves, wells, and mine tailings.

Another theory is that East Lake could have been a long-forgotten terminal of the Underground Railroad, a network of black and white Abolitionists who aided fugitive slaves in their escape to freedom. The Black Cultural Centre is currently investigating that possibility.

Here is some educated guesswork on how Nova Scotia could have become part of the Underground Railroad . . .

In 1850, the United States Congress passed one of the most pernicious and indefensible pieces of legislation in its history: the Fugitive Slave Law. Under that law, owners of escaped slaves were empowered to reclaim their "property" anywhere in the United States, north or south.

Previously, any escaped slave who managed to make his or her way to a state that outlawed slavery was considered free by law. Under the 1850 legislation, though, a fugitive slave could be captured and returned to bondage even in a "free" state. Furthermore, anyone who interfered with the recapture of a slave was liable to face federal charges.

The results of the Fugitive Slave Act were immediate and predictable. Gangs of slave-catchers roamed the cities and hinterland of the North, kidnapping slave and free blacks alike and delivering them to the proverbial "fate worse than death."

For the blacks of that time, the country of their birth had become an even more terrifying place to live. Behind every tree, within every shadow, the slave-catcher lurked like an all-too-real bogeyman.

As well, the Underground Railroad extended its routes north to Canada, where slavery had been abolished in 1834. Most of those routes ended in southern Ontario — then called Upper Canada — by way of Ohio, Pennsylvania, and New York. Black communities were soon established in that area.

Could another, less publicized route have existed, leading to Nova Scotia by way of Boston? It's possible.

Today, some African-Americans are aware of the place Nova Scotia occupies in black history. But they view the province as "the last stop on the Underground Railroad" rather than the destination of the Black Loyalists in 1783 and the Black Refugees in 1814, which preceded the Underground Railroad.

At first glance, that seems to be a misreading of history. Deeper investigation, however, reveals some fascinating hints.

One clue may be found in the celebrated case of Anthony Burns, an escaped slave who was captured in Boston in 1854, and returned to his Virginia owner under the Fugitive Slave Act. Protest against this atrocity was so vehement that 1,500 federal troops were required to escort Burns to the ship that would carry him back to bondage.

Burns' plight was well-known to Father Richard Preston, a fellow Virginian who had come to Nova Scotia four decades earlier and founded the African Baptist Association, forerunner of the current African United Baptist Association. In *A Brief History of the Coloured Baptists of Nova Scotia*, Peter E. McKerrow wrote: "[Preston] felt bad over the return of Burns, a fugitive and countryman of his, who had made his escape to Boston — but for the Fugitive Slave law he would have been clear. 'Poor fellow,' said [Preston], 'should they succeed in getting him back to Virginia, they will torture him.' — which they did. [Preston] knew him well, a Baptist exhorter in Virginia."

Father Preston was also president of the African Abolition Society in Nova Scotia. As such, he could have been the link Abolitionists here and in Boston would have needed to establish an additional Underground Railroad route for New England blacks who feared capture under the Fugitive Slave Law. And the Burns case would have provided added urgency.

Secrecy would have been an absolute necessity. If an oversea Boston-to-Nova Scotia route had become widely known, it would have been a simple matter for authorities and slave-catchers to intercept boatloads of fugitives before they left Boston harbour. Silence was a virtue on the Canadian side as well. As a matter of policy, Canada did not return escaped slaves to the Americans, but slave-catchers were known to slip across the border to abduct blacks for bounty.

Having arrived in Nova Scotia, escapees would have needed a refuge, a place with minimal risk of detection . . . in short, a place like the Preston area, an established but isolated black community in which the fugitives could mingle. It is not difficult to imagine Father Preston convincing the people of the community that bore his name to set aside some land for blacks in need, and to remain silent about the presence of the newcomers.

With the end of the American Civil War in 1865, the need for a secret fugitive slave community in Nova Scotia would have ended as well. The people who lived there could have remained in the area or returned to the United States. And their community, hidden out of necessity, would have been forgotten by all but a few.

Of course, this is all speculation. As a possible missing chapter of Canadian history, though, the East Lake site deserves research, not rubbish.

Garbage dump fight ahead
December 30, 1991

A battle involving the possible desecration of Nova Scotia's black heritage looms in the new year.

The fight involves the three final sites being considered for metro's new landfill. Although media attention has focused on the East Lake site near the Preston area, the other two finalists are located near historically black communities as well. Pockwock, near Hammonds Plains, is close to the Sandy Lake site; and Beechville, which was recently profiled on CBC's First Edition, is near the Big Indian Lake site.

According to the selection criteria, all three communities should be at least three kilometres away from the proposed dump locations. But Pockwock is closer than that to Sandy Lake.

The Metro Authority insists the site-selection process is "color-blind." It's true that the predominantly white communities of Hatchet Lake and Head of St. Margaret's Bay are also near the final sites. Yet all three locations also happen to be close to black communities.

Given the unhappy history involving black communities and garbage dumps in this province, the skepticism of residents of the Prestons, Pockwock, and Beechville isn't hard to understand. The memory of what a city garbage dump did to Africville remains fresh despite the passage of nearly three decades. Another black community on Creighton Avenue in Dartmouth was displaced by a dump as well. The site-selection process in those cases was far from "color-blind." Can the black community of today be faulted for experiencing a sense of *déjà vu* regarding the current landfill controversy?

No community — native, white, black, integrated — looks forward to the presence of a garbage dump in its back yard, even a back yard three to seven kilometres away. Reasons for objecting to landfills, incinerators, and other waste-disposal facilities include political, environmental, aesthetic, economic, and historic factors.

In minority-group communities, the racial factor is deeply involved. Racial minorities have tended to lack the political clout necessary to successfully oppose the implementation of policies that are harmful to them. The fates of Africville and the Creighton Avenue community are stark reminders of the consequences of powerlessness.

But minorities are powerless no longer. Today, you can fight City Hall or Province House or even Parliament Hill, no matter what color you are.

Community leaders in the Preston area are prepared to apply that lesson. Allister Johnson, president of the North Preston Ratepayers Association, has promised a "hard fight" if the East Lake site is chosen. The historic value of the area was discussed in depth yesterday; there are also ecological reasons for resistance to the location of a dump there.

Beechville and Pockwock have also made their opposition clear, as has Head of St. Margaret's Bay.

The final decision on the landfill site will be made at the end of January. Residents near the location that is chosen will protest the outcome. And, like it or not, their protests will include a racial component.

Black history and Site H
February 9, 1992

Recently, *The Daily News* published a letter from Metro Authority Chairman Bill Fenton under the headline: Landfill Site Has No Cultural Value. In defending Site H, or East Lake, near the Preston area, as a location for Metro's newest landfill, Fenton wrote: "The site has been examined and there is no evidence to link the candidate landfill site to early black settlement."

Fenton bases his argument on the assumption of an alleged absence of archaeological, archival, or anecdotal clues pointing toward 19th-century black settlement in the "active" area of the proposed landfill between East Lake and Williams Lake. His letter indicated that the only evidence of such settlement is located either in the landfill's "buffer zone" or beyond the boundaries of the site.

Halifax County Councillor Wayne Adams disagrees.

"There's an old Church map that shows the boundaries of Preston from the shores of Dartmouth to the Myra Road to the airport," says Adams. "That area includes the landfill site. The map's on the wall in the corridor of the County Building. Gerrymandering and redistribution of boundaries doesn't make any difference. It's still an original, black-occupied piece of land."

Concrete, irrefutable evidence of early black occupation of the "active" landfill site remains elusive. There are, however, archival and anecdotal clues that should not be dismissed out of hand by Fenton or anyone else.

One of those clues is the presence of an old family in the area, the Wisdoms. Through archival research, Adams has found that the history of the Wisdoms dates back as far as 1751.

As well, a land grant in the Wisdom name is dated 1781.

The assumption has always been that the Wisdoms were white, primarily because their land holdings totalled 1,000 acres and records list them as employing "servants." It might have been unusual for blacks to have been in that position in the early 1800s — but not impossible.

"I've spoken to some senior citizens who as children knew the Wisdom family," Adams says. "They were very successful farmers and business people, owning apple orchards and a sawmill in the East Lake area. And they are remembered as 'colored folks.'"

One resident of Porter's Lake told Adams the Wisdoms supplied the area with apples and other produce grown in "the landfill site." The same resident also said the Wisdoms were "colored," and he said it in front of a Porter Dillon archaeological consultant who has insisted that the family was white.

"They're trying to make history fit the site," Adams says. "They're trying to reduce the area of black settlement to justify Site H. But the majority of the Wisdoms' 1,000 acres is in the landfill site, and that proves black occupation."

According to Adams' informants, the Wisdoms died out in the 1920s — today's senior citizens remember them as being "elderly" at the time. Whether the Wisdoms were black or white, their legacy recalls a time of hard work and relative racial harmony that has now gone sadly astray.

Another factor Adams considers important was not mentioned in Fenton's letter. "The environmental impact, which they seem to be hiding for some reason or other, goes beyond the history. There are at least seven communities on the Eastern Shore that will be negatively affected if Site H is picked. At last night's (February 4) information meeting, I asked the consultants if there were any guarantees the site won't leak acid leachate. They couldn't make that guarantee."

An acid leachate leak would affect more than just black communities. According to Adams, Lake Echo and Porter's Lake would be polluted "almost immediately," affecting predominantly white areas as well as the Prestons.

Another environmental factor Adams stresses is the need for water resources in an area that has future growth potential. East Lake and Lake Williams form part of the Salmon River Watershed.

"To put a landfill site north of that area, regardless of what they call buffer zones, poses the danger that those bodies of water may not be a good watershed in the future," Adams says. "And to cut off water is to cut off life."

About the only point on which Adams and Fenton agree is Fenton's assertion that "the history of black settlement in this part of Nova Scotia has been poorly documented."

"It's a shame," says Adams, "that historians did not document our history as they did other people's history. On that basis, they should think about removing the site until the history has been thoroughly researched."

Black history has been ignored or denied much too long. As Allister Johnson, president of the North Preston Ratepayers Association puts it: "Who gave this man (Fenton) the right to determine the value of our community and history?"

Who, indeed?

The Metropolitan Authority ultimately selected Site H, or East Lake, as the host of the new landfill. Predictably, the fight intensified.

Site H:
Adding insult to injury
March 15, 1992

In the immediate aftermath of the Metropolitan Authority board's selection of East Lake, or Site H, as the location for a new landfill, the gloves on both sides of the debate are beginning to come off. Opponents of Site H say racism was a factor in the board's decision. Advocates of the site-selection process are taking a more subtle approach.

That subtlety can be seen in some of the comments made to the media in the wake of forceful protests from black community spokesmen.

Allan Smith of the Sackville landfill close-out committee said that opponents of the East Lake site "don't really understand" the realities of the situation. That comment is an insult to the intelligence of the black community — veiled, perhaps, but an insult nonetheless.

Equally derogatory is the suggestion that people whose families have lived in the Prestons for generations do not know the difference between the two East Lakes located in the area.

The charges of racism have placed everyone connected with the site selection on the defensive. Part of their counterattack is to create the impression that their opponents are ignorant and don't know what they're talking about. This impression draws on a stereotype that has been around far longer than the landfill issue.

But when it comes to racism, Nova Scotian blacks —especially those who live in North Preston — do know what they're talking about. To them, the selection of Site H is part of a pattern of persecution that dates back to the year 1815. At that time, the Nova Scotia government was asked by the British to resettle the Black Refugees, American ex-slaves who had escaped to British lines during the War of 1812. A similar migration of Black Loyalists had occurred a generation earlier, at the end of the American Revolution.

Attitudes had changed since then, however, and the province's legislature petitioned Lieutenant-Governor Sherbrooke to ban black immigration. But the will of the British prevailed, and the black newcomers were quarantined at Melville Island, a military prison.

The majority of the Refugees were then offered land in remote areas that held scant agricultural potential. As Allister Johnson of the North Preston Ratepayers Association puts it: "We got the rocks and the natives got the swamps."

Part of those "rocks" became the current location of the Preston communities and Site H. The barren land was essentially a dumping ground for unwanted people. The conventional wisdom at the time must have been that the desolate conditions would drive the Refugees away from the land and into ill-paid positions as laborers and servants.

Instead, the Refugees persevered, and their descendants became the largest indigenous black community in Canada. Along the way, they have had to fight constantly against attempts at relocation and encroachment and for such basic amenities as water and sewer services. They have also contended with negative stereotypes that have been handed down from generation to generation among whites and blacks alike in the rest of Nova Scotia.

Porter Dillon, Ltd., the consultants involved in the selection process, can talk all they want about the 80 "impartial" criteria they employed. But that talk means nothing without taking the 81st criterion into account — the historical pattern that causes the same site to be selected for the dumping of people in the 19th century and garbage in the 20th.

The difference is, people can prosper under the most trying conditions. Garbage just rots.

Now the residents of North Preston are preparing for yet another long, hard struggle. The Metro Authority's decision is hardly a *fait accompli*. A year-long environmental review must be undertaken before the site receives final approval. As well, a CBC First Edition report indicated that the Site H land has not been zoned for industrial use, and suggested that Halifax County Council has the power to kill the entire project by simply refusing to authorize rezoning.

In 1815, the black community's survival was in itself a victory. Today, the battle involves much higher stakes. Its outcome will determine the direction of race relations in this province well into the next century.

Keeping up with the landfill issue
April 26, 1992

If the situation weren't so serious, the past few weeks' worth of developments concerning the East Lake landfill issue would qualify as slapstick comedy.

The misadventures began several weeks ago, when *The Mail-Star* published one of Metro Authority Chairman Bill Fenton's ubiquitous letters to the editor justifying the choice of a site near the Preston communities for the region's latest landfill published in *The Mail-Star*. Along with his usual disclaimers (seven kilometres is a *long* distance and East Lake supposedly has no historical value), Fenton argued the black community has no claim to the site because the land is now owned by the Scott Paper Company.

As if history could be bought and sold like meat cuts in a supermarket . . .

Just because ownership of the East Lake land passed out of the black community's hands, that doesn't mean the site has passed out of its cultural heritage.

Not long after that letter was published, *The Mail-Star* ran a story under this eye-grabbing headline: Scott Vows Battle Over Dump Site. The story indicated that the company would not sell its East Lake holdings to the Metro Authority for purposes that would "... not be beneficial to the long-term betterment of the surrounding communities." And a landfill certainly fits that definition.

Jack Kyte, an executive with Scott Maritimes, was quoted as saying that the subsidiary "would refuse sale and fight expropriation." He also spoke of Scott's "committment to the concerns of the black population."

Naturally, news of Scott's stand boosted spirits in the black communities affected by the landfill decision. But the next day, Kyte told *The Daily News* that Scott wouldn't be fighting expropriation after all.

"We have made no decision to have a major court battle over it," Kyte said. His implication was that it would be impossible to win such a battle.

Strangely, *The Mail-Star* stuck to its original spin on the story, i.e. "corporate giant takes up black community's cause." It appeared that metro's two daily newspapers were reporting stories that were diametrically opposed.

Was Kyte telling *The Mail-Star* one thing and *The Daily News* something else? Was Scott attempting a "double-negative" strategy, in which the company could straddle the fence by refusing to sell the land, but also refusing to fight expropriation?

Referring to Scott's initial announcement on the land sale, East Preston Ratepayers Association president Matthew Thomas was quoted in *The Mail-Star* as saying: "I would hope that this is not just another smokescreen."

But last week, it appeared the smoke was getting thicker by the minute.

In another *Mail-Star* story, Halifax County Warden Laszlo Lichter said the Metro Authority would not put up a fight if Scott Paper opposed expropriation! Why Lichter would say something that after Kyte had already tossed in the towel is one of many unsolved mysteries the landfill issue has generated.

Of course, Lichter isn't chairman of the authority — Bill Fenton is. As yet, Fenton hasn't made any public comment on the matter since his letter to *The Mail-Star.*

Throw in Halifax Mayor Moira Ducharme's controversial endorsement of a proposal to truck metro's trash to a leaky hole in the ground in East Kemptville that was once the Rio Algom tin mine, and what do you get? Something very close to extreme bureaucratic panic.

To be fair to Ducharme, her Rio Algom gambit was more relevant to her opposition to incineration than it was to the East Lake controversy. However, Lichter's hints about refusing to fight a battle he knows he would win are an indication that the Metro Authority may now be thinking twice about its selection of East Lake as the landfill site.

When the decision was made, the authority and its consultants were well aware that charges of racism would arise, and a denial strategy was already locked in place. What the authority didn't anticipate was the local and national support the black community has received. That support has been vocal and broad-based, ranging from the federal government to provincial church and environmental groups.

Instead of weakening in the face of the authority's counter-strategies, opposition to the landfill has increased. Now the politicians and social planners are desperately seeking another solution.

In Lewis Carroll's words from *Alice in Wonderland*, things are getting "curiouser and curiouser."

The vigorous campaign against the East Lake landfill continued through 1992 and the early part of 1993. Finally, the Metro Authority threw in the towel.

What a waste
June 27, 1993

Last Tuesday, the shameful saga of Site H, or East Lake, came to a welcome end when Metropolitan Authority voted 9-1 to rescind its previous decision to place a landfill at that location.

Had objections to Site H been based solely on racial grounds, it is possible Metro Authority might have managed to tough out its decision. Instead of setting blacks against whites in a divide-and-conquer scenario, however, the fight against Site H became a co-operative effort.

Many white residents in the Site H area recognized blacks' historical and cultural concerns. Blacks, in turn, appreciated whites' concentration on environmental issues. The alliance wasn't perfect, but it provided effective opposition to the landfill throughout 1992.

The attacks on Site H came from many perspectives. Blacks from the Preston area argued that an early black settlement — possibly an Underground Railroad settlement for fugitive slaves — had existed in the East Lake area. The Canadian Airline Pilots Association cited a threat from gathering seagulls to planes landing at Halifax International Airport. And Scott Paper, the owner of the Site H land, hinted at an expropriation fight.

45

Earlier this year, the Preston area took its case to the Nova Scotia Human Rights Commission, citing "environmental racism" in the selection of site H. Three members of the former Conservative government — Donald Cameron, Joel Matheson, and Tom McInnis — sided with landfill opponents.

By then, it was clear that politically Site H was simply no longer viable. It was time for Metro Authority to cut its losses and seek an alternative. The clock on the Sackville landfill's end was ticking, and Sackville residents harbored grievances of their own dating back to 1977, when they became the unwilling recipients of Metro's refuse.

Metro Authority then did what it should have done in the first place. It offered a financial compensation package to any community in the area that was willing to host — perhaps a better word is "tolerate" — the landfill.

With the compensation policy in place, Metro Authority considered proposals from Dutch Settlement, Dartmouth, and Sackville. The Dutch Settlement bid, which involves loading ash from the landfill and non-combustible refuse into a gypsum mine at Carrolls Corners, passed Metro Authority's muster last week. And that was the end of the East Lake landfill and the $1 million thus far invested in its development.

However, the story shouldn't end here. The Liberal government ought to call a provincial inquiry to find answers to several questions that have arisen from the entire convoluted process. Those questions include:

Why were all three of the sites on the 1992 short list located close to historically black communities?

Why didn't Metro Authority hold a landfill plebiscite among the communities near the East Lake site, as it did for those near Carrolls Corner?

Why did Metro Authority offer a compensation package to communities that volunteered to accept the landfill after it offered no such deal to the communities on its initial site-selection list?

Why was more than $1 million in taxpayers' money spent in pre-development of Site H in the face of mounting and overwhelming public opposition?

Why did Porter Dillon ignore a Natural Resources Department report citing environmental concerns and a recommendation to designate the site as a protected area?

Why did Porter Dillon flip-flop on its own earlier studies that identified East Lake and Woody Lake as watershed areas unsuited for a landfill?

Why was the black community's contention that the site had historic significance dismissed out of hand?

The results of an official inquiry would ensure that a process that very nearly resulted in disaster need never happen again, and that future Nova Scotian history will not include another Africville — or Sackville — landfill.

Even if an inquiry never occurs, however, the Site H incident is still a turning point for race relations in this province.

Wendell Thomas said it best during a TV interview: "This was a case where people of different communities found a common cause."

Let that be the final lesson and legacy of the controversy.

The East Lake dump story should have ended at that point. But the Metropolitan Authority, in one of its last acts before the province imposed amalgamation on its municipalities, provided a coda.

Site H dump battle continues into 1994
January 2, 1994

In June 1993, Nova Scotia's black community appeared to have won a significant victory. The Metropolitan Authority voted to place the region's new landfill at an abandoned National Gypsum mine in Carroll's Corner, near Dutch Settlement.

Previously, the dump had been slated for East Lake, located near the predominantly black Preston communities. For nearly two years both black and white residents of the area had fought to block the landfill at East Lake, also known as Site H, on cultural and environmental grounds.

When opposition to East Lake reached a high point in 1992, Metro Authority began to cast about for a new site. Last year, residents of Dutch Village voted to accept the landfill at a nearby abandoned mine site in exchange for $2 million in compensation. Incidentally, people in the area near East Lake were not offered the opportunity to vote on the suitability of that site.

At that point, it seemed that the saga of Site H had ended. Not so.

In October, National Gypsum rejected the proposal to place the landfill in its mine. The company had decided it didn't want to risk the possibility of violating future environmental legislation. National Gypsum's U.S. parent company had been retroactively sued in North Carolina and did not want to chance a repeat of history in Nova Scotia.

That decision returned metro's landfill situation to Square One. The existing landfill at Sackville is scheduled to close this year. And the East Lake site has not been decertified.

Thus, the black community's battle over Site H may last well into 1994.

In the end, no garbage dump was located near East Lake. To the dismay of Sackville residents, the life of their landfill was extended for two years. The site finally selected for the Halifax region's new landfill was Otter Lake, an area located near the historically black community of Beechville. Despite the community's objections, the site became operational in 1998.

Racial politics

How Nova Scotia elected its first black MLAs

For many years, the political influence of the Preston area, Nova Scotia's largest black community, was hampered because the area was divided between two provincial ridings. In 1991, the Progressive Conservative government of then premier Donald Cameron proposed a change in electoral boundaries that would place all the Preston area's voters in one riding. Theoretically, that would increase the chances a black candidate could be elected to Province House.

From the beginning, the Preston riding was steeped in controversy.

Wayne Adams, Nova Scotia's first black MLA, greets his successor, Yvonne Atwell, on night of March 1998 election. *(Sandor Fizli/The Daily News)*

Political affirmative action
April 29, 1991

Premier Donald Cameron's endorsement of a proposed redrawing of provincial electoral boundaries in Halifax County is a welcome development. The change would create a riding containing most of the black population in the Preston, Lake Echo, and Lake Loon area. Estimates of that population's size range from 6,000 to 8,000.

The black riding idea comes on the heels of an earlier proposal for the establishment of an "at-large" provincial legislature seat for the Mi'kmaq. An "at-large" seat would not be confined to a specific geographical area, but it would still represent Nova Scotia's Native population in unprecedented fashion.

Cameron supports the latter notion as well. Will his support lead to implementation? That remains to be seen.

There are some who would consider both ideas a form of political affirmative action. The concept of affirmative action has aroused controversy throughout its existence because of the multitude of misconceptions that surround it.

The main misconception is that affirmative action amounts to discrimination against white people. Applying that argument to the black and Mi'kmaq political proposals, two Province House seats occupied by minority-group members equals two seats that rightfully belong to whites. To whom do the rest of the seats "rightfully" belong?

In reality, the proposed Preston and Mi'kmaq seats would serve to diminish discrimination against minorities. No longer would Mi'kmaq and black votes be scattered all over the province like drops in 50 different buckets. Voters would be empowered to vote for a person to represent their concerns at Province House. To such an MLA, the interests of his or her constituents would be paramount, not superseded by those of the majority.

The color of that representative's skin would be irrelevant. If the voters of a Preston-area riding decided to elect a white or Asian or Lebanese MLA, that would be their prerogative. If they decided to elect Nova Scotia's first black MLA, that would also be up to them.

There is, however, one caveat to consider. Although an at-large Mi'kmaq seat would theoretically represent all natives in Nova Scotia, a

Preston-area MLA would have a mandate to speak only for the blacks of that riding. For blacks in the rest of the province, the old game of marshalling minuscule clout to maximum effect would continue. And that game is extremely difficult to win. But that's no reason to deny a political voice to the largest concentration of indigenous blacks in Canada.

Cynics might downplay the importance of a lone black or Mi'kmaq MLA sitting in Province House. As single voices among a chorus of others singing on a different key, what practical political significance would those members have? Would their value be more symbolic than real?

Perhaps those questions should be directed to Manitoba MLA Elijah Harper, who is now the best-known provincial backbencher in Canada. Harper, who is of Cree extraction and represents a riding created especially for Natives in the northern part of Manitoba, provided an object lesson in parliamentary procedure when he helped to sink the Meech Lake Accord last year.

Last March 21, Premier Cameron provided the opening address for the International Day for the Elimination of Racial Discrimination. In his speech, the premier expressed deep concern over the negative effects of racism. He also recognized the need for concrete action to eradicate discrimination based on skin color and other racial characteristics.

This is the type of rhetoric one would expect to hear from any politician on such an occasion. However, Cameron's public statements on the Preston re-districting and the Mi'kmaq at-large seat are much more than rhetoric. His support for reforms that probably don't sit too well with his peers indicates a genuine commitment to the cause of racial equality.

Let's see if he can convince his colleagues to do the right thing before the next election. There may never be a better chance than now to welcome minorities into the halls of political power — for better or worse.

Local blacks become political
October 14, 1991

Last week, the provincial commission on electoral boundaries heard several suggestions concerning ways to increase the political clout of the people of the Prestons/Cherry Brook area, which is Nova Scotia's — and Canada's — largest concentration of indigenous blacks. Unfortunately, this issue has become confused with the question of how to elect the province's first black MLA, which is a different matter altogether.

Until now, the Prestons/Cherry Brook community has been divided between two provincial ridings. This division has diluted the area's political influence. To combine those communities into a single riding — or, more accurately, part of a single riding — would be nothing more than a matter of recognizing its historic integrity. The same principle would apply to any community, regardless of the color of its residents.

In fact, the proportion of black voters in the proposed new riding would be somewhere between one-fourth and one-third of the total population — hardly sufficient to ramrod a candidate into office on a strictly racial basis.

If the voters of the proposed riding wanted to elect a black MLA to represent them, that would be their privilege. If they wanted to elect a white or Native MLA that, too, would be their privilege. The relevant factor here is that a community united by history would no longer be divided by an arbitrary political boundary.

As far as the matter of a black MLA is concerned, who says he or she would necessarily have to be elected in a riding with a large black population? The previous best hope for a black MLA came during the 1988 provincial election, when former Annapolis Royal Mayor Daurene Lewis made a strong but unsuccessful showing for the Liberals. The riding she contested has a relatively small black population. Yet she still came close to election. For all we know, Nova Scotia's first black MLA could come from Pictou County.

The confusion of the two issues — the political reunification of the Prestons/Cherry Brook and the election of a black MLA — has resulted in yet another pointless debate over "quotas" and "reverse discrimination." Some critics have complained that the creation of a designated "black seat" will lead to further polarization of the races.

Yet the advocates of the redrawn boundaries, including County Councillor Wayne Adams, Howard Williams, Jr., Wendell Thomas, and Rev. Darryl Gray, have unanimously rejected the notion of a special "black seat" in the Nova Scotia legislature.

The "black seat" critics could benefit from a look back at the recent political history of District 8 in Halifax County, a district that includes the Prestons area. Wayne Adams has been county councillor for that district since 1979. Adams's immediate predecessor was Patrick LaChance, who was white.

Any suggestion that the people of this area will "automatically" vote for a black candidate on purely racial grounds is a serious underestimation of — and insult to — their intelligence.

The Electoral Boundaries Commission eventually created the Preston riding, in which approximately one-third of the voters were black. In 1993, the governing Progressive Conservatives called an election. The Preston riding became one of the most closely watched contests on voting day.

Race and a riding
May 23, 1993

In the fall of 1991, a provincial commission on electoral boundaries conducted hearings to receive input from the public on how the province's ridings should be redrawn in the wake of the latest census. Two of the issues the commission considered were the establishment of special seats to guarantee representation of blacks and Mi'kmaq at Province House.

After a lengthy and sometimes acrimonious debate, the idea of special seats was set aside. However, the commission did recommend the creation of a riding to be called Preston. Not only would this new riding consolidate the voting power of the Preston-Cherry Brook black communities, which had previously been split between two ridings; it would also mean blacks would constitute approximately one-third of the new riding's population.

In the spring of 1992, the provincial legislature passed the commission's recommendation, and the Preston riding was born. Its name evoked black history. Although the area was not named for Rev. Richard Preston, it served as home base for that renowned 19th-century black churchman.

However, a variety of perceptions concerning the Preston riding's purpose have led to controversy that could continue well beyond this Tuesday's election. In the minds of some members of the public and the media, the idea of a designated black riding did not stay dead after the electoral boundaries commission killed it last year.

At first, the line on the Preston riding was that its population mix would provide the blacks in the area greater say in deciding their representation in Province House. That changed to: "This is the best opportunity yet for the election of a black MLA." Then perceptions changed again to: "This is the black riding," an impression that prevails in some minds regardless of population statistics.

In fact, some commentators have called the riding an example of "racial gerrymandering" because of its higher black population. What label did they use when the black population in the old riding was less than 10 per cent?

At the time the riding was formed, the Conservatives' mandate had little more than a year remaining. An election call seemed imminent, and the search for candidates in all ridings heated up.

Most of the candidates who came forward to seek nomination for the Preston riding were black. Halifax County Councillor Wayne Adams won the Liberals' nomination by acclamation. Yvonne Atwell took the NDP's nomination by one vote over Allister Johnson. And Rev. Darryl Gray won the Conservatives' nod.

It was the Tories' nomination battle that made the most headlines. Initially, the contestants for the nomination included Gray, Betty Thomas, and David Hendsbee, a former aide to Deputy Premier Tom McInnis.

Hendsbee was the only white candidate to run for any of the three parties' nominations. He is a native of the area, and has long been involved in its political and social causes. However, he had also been fired from his position as McInnis's aide for his role in the leaking of a confidential tax list for a Tory fund-raising letter.

Premier Don Cameron announced that if Hendsbee won the nomination, he would refuse to sign the candidate's nomination papers. Hendsbee dropped out of the race, and Gray won the nomination. Later, Hendsbee announced that he would run as an independent candidate, thus pitting three blacks from the established parties against one white outsider.

Ironically, three of the four candidates — Adams, Gray and Hendsbee — had made presentations to the Electoral Boundaries Commission. Now, events had conspired to produce the Commission's worst nightmare: a racial campaign.

In the final days before the election, the candidates are footsore and confident, tired but still willing to share their thoughts. I interviewed all four of them over the telephone last week, and the results are presented in alphabetical order.

Liberal nominee Wayne Adams sees this election as the culmination of a process that began two decades ago.

"(Liberal MLA) A. Garnet Brown presented a private member's bill regarding the creation of a Preston riding back in 1976," Adams says. "Premier Cameron didn't make history with his endorsement of the riding. He only revived an old idea."

Adams has been District 8 county councillor since 1979, and is well known in the riding. But he's still knocking on doors well into the night. "I'm getting a good feeling at those doors," he says. "There's clear support for me, and a lot fewer undecideds than you'd expect."

Polls show Adams holding the lead over his rivals. Still, in his 1991 county council bid, he was held to a narrow victory in a four-person race. That result implies a vulnerability the other candidates might exploit.

For NDP candidate Yvonne Atwell, the election presents two challenges. The first is to raise the profile of a party that has had little impact in the Preston area. "When I started, my campaign was totally dismissed," she says. "It took lots of hard work just to become recognized as a serious candidate."

Her other challenge is to counteract her image as a black radical. That image developed through media attention drawn by her work with the Black United Front and the Afro-Canadian Caucus. Atwell is using reality to confront perception.

"When I go white voters' doors, I get a positive reaction," she says. "Especially from women. Also, most of the people on my campaign committee are white."

The NDP faces an uphill fight in the Preston riding. Atwell is running uphill as hard as she can.

P.C. candidate Darryl Gray gives the impression he'll be happy whether he wins or loses the election.

"The level of participation in the process is so much higher now," he says. "People from nine to 90 are involved."

Gray has had to battle image problems of his own. Cameron recently refused to sign nomination papers for Paddy Fitzgerald, a convicted — and pardoned — rapist. Gray, on the other hand, was convicted on marijuana and break-and-enter charges in the United States.

If Cameron signed Gray's nomination papers, why wouldn't he sign Fitzgerald's?

"There's a world of difference between our cases," Gray says. "I was a youth when I was convicted; Mr. Fitzgerald was a mature, accomplished barrister. Also, Premier Cameron recognized that there is bias against blacks in the U.S. justice system."

Gray has established close ties with Cameron. On that basis, he will sink or swim in the election.

As the only white candidate contesting the Preston riding, David Hendsbee bridles at any suggestion that his campaign is racially motivated.

"Out of the 11 people who signed my nominating petition, five were blacks," he says. "There's no reason for anyone to think I wouldn't represent everyone in this riding, regardless of race."

Hendsbee doesn't view his independent status as a handicap.

"All MLAs have service budgets," he says. "There's a lot I could do for the constituency without having to be a party member."

Hendsbee does, however, show a bit of defensiveness regarding the racial aspect of the campaign.

"There's intimidation going on," he says. "Some people who support me might decide not to do so openly for fear of being called racists. That's a subversion of the democratic process."

We'll see about that on May 25.

The Liberals won the election in a landslide, taking 39 of the province's 51 ridings. The Conservatives finished with nine seats and the NDP three. Wayne Adams won the Preston riding.

Preston:
Voting math is food for thought
May 30, 1993

Although the Preston riding provided plenty of thrills on election night, the outcome was predictable. Long-time County Councillor Wayne Adams won the newly created seat for the Liberals, taking 38 per cent of the vote. Independent David Hendsbee, the only white candidate in the contest, was runner-up with 29 per cent. Conservative candidate Darryl Gray finished third with 21 per cent, and the NDP's Yvonne Atwell brought up the rear with 12 per cent.

That's the order many observers foresaw. In a four-way race that featured strong candidates, Adams's victory was solid, though nowhere near the tidal wave his party achieved throughout the province. And at this point it would be easy to say history has been made with the election of Nova Scotia's first black MLA, and leave it at that.

However, a closer look at the riding's arithmetic reveals some fascinating elements that could have a bearing on future elections.

First, the racial breakdown of the riding's population is approximately two-thirds white and one-third black. But in the election, 71 per cent of the Preston voters chose one of the three black candidates, while 29 per cent voted for Hendsbee. This result suggests that race was not as large a factor in voters' minds once they entered the voting booths as it appeared to have been during door-to-door campaigning.

Voting patterns in individual polls reinforce that suggestion. Of the 23 polls in the riding, Adams won 13, Hendsbee seven, and Gray three. Adams also won the advance poll. Atwell had to be content with third-place finishes in more than half the polls.

An analysis of the polling stations, which were located in predominantly black, predominantly white and racially mixed areas of the riding, provides the true anatomy of the returns.

The most striking result came from the three North Preston Recreation Centre polls. To put it bluntly, Darryl Gray kicked serious behind in North Preston, winning 76 per cent of the vote. Adams trailed badly with 19 per cent. Atwell received three per cent; Hendsbee got two per cent. In one of the area's polls, Hendsbee didn't get a single vote.

North Preston gave Gray 43 per cent of his total vote count. Without that bulge, he would have been in a tight battle with Atwell for third place overall.

The overwhelming rejection of Hendsbee in North Preston could be interpreted by some as a racial vote. But that theory doesn't explain why those same voters also rejected Atwell and Adams, both of whom are black.

At any rate, Gray's showing in North Preston was something of a moral victory, and stamps him as a politician to be reckoned with in the future.

Adams's home area of East Preston came through strongly for him, giving him 55 per cent of the vote in its two polling stations at the East Preston Recreation Centre. Gray came second with a respectable 31 per cent. Atwell and Hendsbee trailed at nine and five per cent respectively.

Lake Echo Fire Hall's four polling stations were in a predominantly white area. Hendsbee's campaign office was located there, and post-election media reports said he gained much of his vote count there. Not so, according to the figures. Adams took 41 per cent of the vote at the Lake Echo polls. Hendsbee managed 36 per cent. Atwell got 14 per cent and Gray trailed with nine.

The four stations at St. John's Hall drew voters from white and black communities alike, including Cherry Brook and Lake Loon. Adams won handily there, taking 40 per cent of the vote to Hendsbee's 30. Atwell and Gray split the remainder at 15 per cent each.

The areas covered by the rest of the riding's polling stations — Humber Park School, St. Mark's Hall and St. Anne's Hall — were predominantly white. In those 10 polls, Adams and Hendsbee finished in a dead heat at 38 per cent apiece. Atwell came third with 14 per cent and Gray barely broke double digits with 10 per cent.

Among the conclusions that can be drawn from these numbers are the following:

Wayne Adams' victory was broad-based, with substantial support from voters of both races.

Despite Adams' crossover appeal, the Conservatives might have won the seat had they been united behind one candidate.

A divided black vote doesn't necessarily lead to a defeated black candidate.

The New Democratic Party has a great deal of work to do in the riding.

White voters in the Preston riding will vote for black candidates, and they will also vote for a white candidate without worrying about being labeled racist.

History has been made. Now, let's hope that in the next provincial election, the Preston riding doesn't receive any more attention than the other 51 in the province.

Most Nova Scotians accepted Adams' victory and recognized its significance. The Globe and Mail, however, begged to differ.

Canada's irrational newspaper
July 12, 1993

When, oh when, will *The Globe and Mail's* editorial writers get off Wayne Adams's case and accept the legitimacy of his election as Nova Scotia's first black MLA?

On May 25, Adams made history when he won the newly created Preston riding for the Liberals. Later, Premier John Savage named him Minister of Supply and Services.

Within days of the election, *The Globe* published an editorial that questioned the manner in which the Preston riding was formulated. Citing its small population and large (one-third) proportion of black voters, *The Globe* accused Nova Scotia of creating an "electoral ghetto" in the riding, thus diminishing the validity of Adams' win.

This narrow-minded view of the election was duly criticized by provincial NDP Leader Alexa McDonough in a letter to *The Globe*, and also in this space. That should have been the end of the matter.

Unfortunately, it's not over yet.

Earlier this month, in an editorial headlined Gerrymandering by Race and Place, *The Globe* discussed a U.S. Supreme Court decision that upheld objections to the boundaries of the 12th Congressional District in North Carolina.

The district in question stretches snakelike over about 250 kilometres along the I-85 highway. The boundary was drawn that way to ensure that the majority of voters in the district would be black. In the 1992 U.S.

elections, Melvin Watt, a black man, won the district. A black woman, Eva Clayton, was elected in another district that was not challenged. Watt and Clayton were the first blacks to be elected to Congress from North Carolina in 91 years.

Then five dissatisfied white voters from Watt's district mounted a court challenge to its boundaries, arguing that its majority-black population violated white interests. By a narrow 5-4 decision, the U.S. Supreme Court ruled in favor of the complainants. Justice Sandra Day O'Connor, author of the majority's opinion, wrote that race-based redistricting "bears an uncomfortable resemblance to political apartheid." The ruling has not invalidated the concept of districts with so-called "minority majorities." But it served notice that boundaries in such districts should not be gerrymandered, or drawn with a hidden agenda in mind.

The Globe's editorial agreed with the U.S. ruling. Then it went on to compare its circumstances to the "remarkable but little-noticed inequities" in Canadian electoral ridings.

For an example of such an inequity, *The Globe* chose its favorite whipping boy, Wayne Adams, drawing the following comparison between the Nova Scotia and North Carolina situations: "In a May general election in Nova Scotia, the province elected its first black MLA. Good. But two aspects of his election are troubling. The borders of the riding which Liberal Wayne Adams represents were purposely drawn to encompass the largest possible number of black voters. And in the interest of increasing the voting strength of this population, this riding was also permitted to be the least populous in the province. The votes of its residents carry more weight than those of other voters."

Essentially, *The Globe* is saying that if the U.S. Supreme Court were ruling on the Preston riding, it would come to the same conclusion it did regarding the 12th North Carolina District. But the comparison is fallacious. Unlike the 12th District, the Preston riding does not have a majority black population. Instead of artificially creating a "minority majority," the provincial electoral boundaries commission enhanced a minority's voting power.

As for the riding's population size: it may be the smallest, but others, such as Clare, aren't that much larger. Do they also represent "inequity" in *The Globe's* eyes?

Nova Scotians have accepted — and even applauded — Adams's election win. Why can't Canada's national newspaper do the same?

Adams was later moved from the Supply and Services department to Environment, and remained at the head of that department until the March 1998 provincial election, in which he was favored to retain his seat.

Preston race matters
March 22, 1998

In 1993, the contest for the newly formed Preston riding was arguably the most closely watched race in the provincial election — and rightly so. This year, the riding has made no headlines — again, rightly so.

The reason all eyes were on Preston then was that the riding was created to consolidate the votes of the area's black communities. The riding was controversial well before the election. Misguided critics said a minority-enhanced riding was "racist" because the black vote was boosted. But blacks account for, at most, one-third of the riding's vote.

If anything, the ensuing campaign in the riding was more controversial than its birth. The Liberals nominated Wayne Adams. Yvonne Atwell won the NDP nod.

The Conservatives provided the thrills. Darryl Gray, a preacher-politician, ran for the Tory nomination. So did David Hendsbee, a Conservative party official. But then premier Donald Cameron said he would not sign Hendsbee's nomination papers because of a list-leaking incident. Gray won the nomination. Hendsbee ran as an independent.

Adams won handily to become Nova Scotia's first black MLA. Hendsbee finished second, Gray third and Atwell fourth.

Since then, the lives of the candidates in that historic election have taken different turns. Hendsbee is a councillor for the Halifax Regional Municipality. Gray continued in his roles as minister and community activist. Recently, he accepted a post as minister for a church in Montreal. Atwell is director of the African Canadian Employment Clinic. In 1996, she ran a losing race for the leadership of the provincial NDP. Once again, she is contesting the Preston riding.

Adams has held two cabinet portfolios — Supply and Services, and Environment. He has done well in both posts, although not without a few stumbles, including a disagreement over whether a new 10-cent deposit on drink containers is a tax, and an accusation of interference in the location of a tire-recycling plant. He emerged relatively unscathed from those conflicts.

This year, Adams faces only two rivals: Atwell of the NDP and Ross Isenor of the Progressive Conservatives. Isenor is a retired Defence Department employee. Although Isenor is white, the race element is absent from this year's campaign. A recent Omnifacts poll indicated that Adams was only "slightly ahead" of Atwell.

Adams and his fellow Liberals are not in the same kind of trouble the Conservatives were in during the 1993 election, when voters wanted to turf the Tories at all costs. The Preston contest pits Adams's long record of service against Atwell's activism and an NDP resurgence. Isenor is decidedly a dark horse.

The absence of racial unrest is the main reason the Preston riding is off the media radar screens. This time, the seat will be decided on the candidates' merits, as it should be.

Overall, the election resulted in a tie between the Liberals and New Democrats, each winning 19 seats. The Conservatives took 14. Several Grit cabinet ministers went down to defeat — including Wayne Adams.

Atwell goes from last to first in Preston vote
April 5, 1998

For two provincial elections in a row, voters in the Preston riding have made history. In 1993, they elected Liberal Wayne Adams as Nova Scotia's first black MLA. Adams finished first in a four-way race, ahead of independent David Hendsbee, Progressive Conservative Darryl Gray and the NDP's Yvonne Atwell. He later held the Supply and Services and Environment cabinet portfolios.

However, the combined votes for Gray and spurned-Tory Hendsbee were more than Adams's tally, suggesting that a unified Conservative party might have taken the seat.

Last month, Preston voters chose Atwell as the province's first black woman MLA — at Adams's expense.

In a remarkable last-place-to-winner's-circle turnaround, Atwell garnered 43 per cent of the 4,135 votes cast in the riding — nearly 10 points higher than the NDP's overall provincial score. Adams came second with 37 per cent. Tory candidate Ross Isenor trailed with 20 per cent.

Atwell's victory was part of the big breakthrough the NDP achieved in metro Halifax ridings, primarily at the expense of the Grits. Adams, in turn, was a victim of the anti-Grit backlash that pushed five fellow cabinet ministers out of office.

Also, as environment minister, Adams was associated with, if not responsible for, several unpopular and controversial matters, including the delisting and relisting of Jim Campbells Barren as a protected ecological site; the location of metro's new landfill; and the cleanup of the Sydney tar ponds. Adams's long service as the area's county councillor and MLA was not enough to overcome the voters' desire for change.

Overall, the Grits and NDP tied with 19 seats each, and 14 went to the Conservatives.

Atwell ran a tough, smart, grassroots-oriented campaign. As well, she augmented her profile in 1996 with her quixotic run against Robert Chisholm for the provincial NDP leadership.

Isenor was not a factor. He was nominated on March 6; the election was March 24. Also, the Tories as a whole were weak in metro.

In contrast to the 1993 election, race played no role in this campaign, even though Isenor is white and Adams and Atwell black. Voting patterns reflected the back seat to which racial matters were relegated.

Overall, in 1993 Adams won 13 of 23 polls in the riding, followed by seven for Hendsbee and three for Gray. Atwell came no higher than third in any of the polls.

This year, Atwell took 14 of 22 polls. Adams won six. Two were tied between Atwell and Adams.

North Preston's polls went solidly for Gray in 1993, giving him 76 per cent of their votes. This year, voters there switched their allegiance to Adams, giving him 65 per cent to Atwell's 31. Isenor trailed with four per cent. The race was tighter in East Preston. There, Adams took 49 per cent of the ballots, with Atwell close behind at 46 per cent. Isenor had five per cent.

The North and East Preston polls are mostly black. Lake Echo's polls are in predominantly — but not overwhelmingly — white areas. Atwell won those polls handily with 45 per cent of the vote, compared with Adams's 33 and Isenor's 22. In 1993, the numbers there were: Adams, 41 per cent; Hendsbee 36; Atwell 14; Gray nine.

In the rest of the riding's polls, in which the racial breakdown reflects that of the riding as a whole — two-thirds white, one-third black — Atwell won 42 per cent of the vote, Adams 32 per cent and Isenor 26 per cent. The 1993 breakdown was Adams and Hendsbee in a dead heat at 38 per cent each, followed by Atwell with 14 per cent and Gray's 10 per cent.

The 1998 results suggest that with Gray and Hendsbee out of the contest, race played only a minimal role this year.

Congratulations are due to Atwell, who overcame the closed doors of 1993 to walk through the doors of Province House in 1998. Condolences are offered to Adams, who fought the good fight, but was unable to withstand the orange NDP crush in metro. Condolences are also due to Isenor, who was put in the impossible position of running a three-week campaign against two formidable adversaries.

And congratulations to all three candidates for keeping the race card in the deck this time out.

Atwell was named the NDP's critic for business and consumer services and the status of women. Adams accepted a position with a Halifax public-relations firm. Not long after the election, racial controversy was raised once again .

Atwell isn't advocating segregation
June 7, 1998

When Yvonne Atwell won the Preston riding to become Nova Scotia's first black woman MLA, she made history. And when she stood up in Province House to speak in response to the throne speech, she made waves.

"I believe that I have seen a very dangerous, and sometimes a very racist and inappropriate, behavior exhibited in this House in the past, in the sense that the sole African-Nova Scotian MLA was looked to as the unofficial minister of African-Nova Scotian affairs," Atwell said.

"I believe it is unacceptable, in this day and age, to expect one African-Nova Scotian person to represent the needs and desires of the entire African-Nova Scotian community spread across 27 communities. A way must be found to allow these people to participate in the selection of an individual who will give voice to their issues and concerns."

She suggested the establishment of a "dedicated seat" for black Nova Scotians as a solution to the problem.

Atwell also expressed concerns over lack of black representation on school boards that have been restructured through amalgamation. That issue was lost in the furore her comments on provincial politics ignited.

Daily News columnist Nancy Radcliffe came close to accusing Atwell of advocating segregation, and of believing that "white MLAs cannot adequately represent black constituents."

Harry Flemming, another *Daily News* columnist, said Atwell "wants to institutionalize racism."

Of 66 callers and e-mailers who responded to a *Daily News* Hotline question on a designated seat for blacks, 63 were against the idea. One caller went so far as to suggest Atwell resign her seat "if she thinks that she must represent blacks."

But Atwell never said she "must represent blacks." In her speech in the House, she said: "Although I indicated that I want to bring an African-Nova Scotian perspective to the House, I want to clearly point out that I fully recognize and accept the fact that my community is very diverse. Unlike previous politicians, I intend to represent the interests of all my constituents. There will be no group within the Preston riding who shall remain without a champion or who will remain voiceless."

A few days later, Atwell said in the House: "I feel that all the people within my constituency, be it North Preston, East Preston, Wonderland Trailer Park, Porter's Lake North, Lake Echo, these are all my communities."

It is precisely because she does not wish to be put in the position of representing all blacks in the province that Atwell suggested the "dedicated" seat.

Soon after she won the Preston riding in the March 24 election, Atwell began to receive calls from black people in other ridings.

"They asked me to help them because they didn't trust their own MLAs," she says. "They thought I could better understand their problems. In some cases, they said they just didn't feel comfortable talking to a white person."

That's why Atwell proposed the "dedicated seat," knowing exactly what kind of reaction that suggestion would get. It was her solution to the dilemma she faced: how to represent her own diverse constituency while at the same time functioning as an unofficial "at-large" representative for all black Nova Scotians — or, at least, the ones who cannot bring themselves to talk to their own MLAs.

Atwell scoffs at the notion that she is promoting segregation.

"Anyone who thinks that doesn't understand the facts," she says. "It's not segregation at all. It's a matter of choice. Segregation is a forced situation."

Other minority communities, such as the Acadians and the Mi'kmaq, have been offered their own representation, Atwell says. "And you never hear a word about segregation with them."

Atwell says that because of historic patterns of discrimination against Nova Scotia's black community, a dedicated seat is needed "to allow structurally for African Nova Scotians' interests to be adequately represented" in Province House. The Preston riding does not, and cannot, serve that purpose for all blacks in the province.

I agree with Atwell in principle. In practice, however, such a seat would end up being more trouble than the struggle necessary to obtain it would be worth.

Any person elected to a dedicated black seat would be so occupied fending off the assaults of all the Harry Flemmings and Hotliners in Nova Scotia that he or she wouldn't have the time or energy to represent the black community's interests.

Still, Atwell raises an important concern: why do some black Nova Scotians feel so ill-served by non-black representatives that they don't even feel free to talk with them?

And if Atwell's suggestion of a dedicated black seat isn't the solution, then what is?

It's easy to throw around words like "segregation" and "institutionalized racism" in reference to suggestions such as Atwell's. It's not so easy to come up with other alternatives.

The only ones I can think of are redoubling efforts to get more black candidates to run in provincial elections, and educating white MLAs about the concerns of blacks and other minorities to allow them to better represent all their constituents. No constituents should ever have any reason to avoid talking to their MLA.

But is that enough? If it isn't, then Atwell's proposal will not go away anytime soon.

Bagpiper Jermaine Downey salutes during dedication of RCMP office at the Black Cultural Centre for Nova Scotia. *(Darrell Oake/The Daily News)*

What's going on

From the battle against drugs to the struggle to save an institution

Cole Harbour High, the East Lake landfill, and the Preston riding were not the only major issues black Nova Scotians have faced in recent years. The battle against racism in this province has been fought on other fronts as well, ranging from the details of day-to-day living to the long-range policies of the provincial and municipal governments; from the classroom to the courtroom; from individual encounters to collective bargaining.

The following is a look at other issues and events that have affected Black Bluenosers during the last decade of the 20th century. Repercussions from some of these events will continue well beyond the year 2000.

Fight for a neighborhood
November 25, 1990

During the late 1980s, decay and doom were the adjectives most frequently used to describe inner cities throughout North America. As economic conditions deteriorated, crime and violence increased exponentially. Much of this increase was related to a virtual epidemic in the use of such addictive drugs as crack cocaine, heroin, and others.

Halifax's North End community was, and to an extent still is, perceived as a small-scale version of the type of inner-city neighborhood that breeds fear in Toronto, Montreal, New York, and Los Angeles. Drug-dealing in the streets, drug-related robbery and prostitution, and "crack babies" became the symbols of the community. The struggling, law-abiding residents who had to live with those problems were ignored by government and the media.

Yet the problems were real, and getting worse. Something had to be done.

In 1988, a self-help group called Concerned Citizens Against Drugs organized in response to tension caused by two drug-related murders in the beleaguered North End. CCAD's founders included Joan Jones, Ricky Anderson, Lorne Izzard, Sandra Downey, Melinda Daye, and others who either lived in or had close ties with the North End community.

Their concern encompassed more than just the killings; they were well aware of the social and economic context in which these and other drug-related problems occurred. That context became the focus of CCAD's efforts.

By 1989, the group had received funding from Health and Welfare Canada to provide anti-drug education and counselling. Later this month, CCAD will learn whether or not its federal funding will be renewed. According to CCAD's chairman, Cecil Wright, the group's services will be "extremely difficult" to maintain without government help, as private and corporate contributions are "almost nil."

"We've tried everything," says Wright. "Pepsi Cola has a foundation that's supposed to be giving out a million dollars for organizations, I thought such as ours, who are doing community-based work to keep people drug-free. We haven't gotten a dime. We have an application pending with United Way, but haven't heard anything yet. We do get volunteers, and their work is valuable and appreciated. But we need full-time staff, too. And full-time staff has to be paid."

Currently, CCAD has one full-time staff member — program director Quenta Adams. There is also a secretary/administrative assistant. As well, a professional drug therapist from the Nova Scotia Commission on Drug Dependency works out of CCAD's Gottingen Street office three days a week.

Adams, who has interrupted her university education to work for CCAD, wears many hats during a typical day at the office. Her duties include telephone and face-to-face counselling, setting up support groups for youths and adults, and giving lectures at schools. The office averages approximately 10 new contacts a day, and Adams estimates that about three-quarters of those who seek help at CCAD will return for further support.

"Most people who drop in or call in don't start off talking about drugs," says Adams. "They'll talk about personal problems or problems on the job. Sooner or later, they'll get around to what's really bothering them. We don't pry or push. We just let them know we're there for them, and can help them when they're ready to accept help."

For all the assistance CCAD offers, however, its ultimate goal is to see the community working independently to rid itself of the drug problem.

"We don't want people to become totally dependent on us," says Adams. "We encourage the formation of independent peer and parental support groups. We start such groups up and provide resources for them. But they set their own agendas."

Although public perception tends to view the drug problem primarily as a black problem, CCAD is not an exclusively black organization. Non-blacks are involved in CCAD's activities, and its services are available to anyone, regardless of race, color, or creed.

Still, a great deal of CCAD's energy is directed toward the black community in the North End of Halifax. The reason for that focus is the black community's vulnerability to the effects of drugs or any other social problem. Unemployment, educational disadvantages, and family breakdown contribute to this vulnerability, in the same way that extreme stress contributes to the human body's susceptibility to disease.

CCAD's profile became significantly expanded after a 1989 rally at the North Branch Library following the drug-related murder of Bernard

Gray. At that meeting, both Mayor Ron Wallace and then police chief Blair Jackson came under heavy fire from North End residents. Many considered Gray's death a symptom of the city's indifference to the plight of the community.

As a result of that concern, HPD established an office in the area. Wright believes that office has helped to prevent the drug problem from becoming worse. But he doesn't think an increased police presence has ended the problem.

"Education is my big platform," says Wright. "If we can educate these young kids when they're 15 or 16, they won't be making those irresponsible decisions to get themselves in a position where they'll be harmfully affected by drugs."

On the whole, CCAD's image in the community has been a positive one. There are, however, some dissenters. According to Wright, there are some who refer to CCAD as "a bunch of snitches" out to "finger" people to turn over to the police.

"We're concerned people trying to make a difference in society, trying to save people's lives," says Wright. "I don't think anybody who's doing anything respectable would have any need to refer to us as 'snitches.'"

What, then, has CCAD accomplished over the two years of its existence? Has the organization made a difference?

Both Wright and Adams believe it has.

"I would think people's fears aren't quite as high as they were two years ago," says Wright. "However, I would also say the problem hasn't subsided, as some people would want us to believe."

Adams agrees. "The problem itself hasn't gotten better," she says. "But it hasn't got worse, and that's the important thing. People in the community are more aware of what the drug problem is, and what steps can be taken to prevent it. That goes especially for younger people."

CCAD represents a practical, grassroots approach to a problem that adds one more hurt to a community that's been hurting for a long time. Its current budget is approximately $55,000 — less than the salary of most business executives or professionals. It deserves the support of everyone. When all is said and done, aren't most of us "concerned citizens against drugs?"

Charlie Zone:
Skirting around race issue
August 30, 1992

The Charlie Zone police office was hailed as a breakthrough in community-based policing when it opened on Gottingen Street two years ago. North End Halifax residents, incensed over a spate of drug-related shootings during the late 1980s, demanded better police protection in their area. The establishment of the Charlie Zone office was viewed as a response to that demand.

Until recently, Charlie Zone rode a wave of positive publicity. Media reports, including an article on the North End published in a recent issue of *Canadian Geographic*, extolled the positive connection the officers stationed there were making with North End residents. Charlie Zone's effect on the crime rate was more difficult to establish, but apparently progress was at least beginning there as well.

Recently, though, Charlie Zone's image has taken a turn for the worse. Its windows have been broken, and unignited Molotov cocktails have flown through its doors. The residents the office was intended to protect have complained that it's open only during business hours Monday to Friday, not nights and weekends when it's needed most.

Last week, a pair of front-page stories in *The Chronicle-Herald/Mail-Star* suggested that "politics" is preventing police from doing their jobs in the Gottingen Street area. In a related matter, a Halifax Police Department official said crime statistics for the area aren't released because they are too "politically sensitive" to be made public.

More specifically, Inspector Larry Clare of HPD's records department told *The Herald* that Alderman Graham Downey, whose ward includes Gottingen Street, "doesn't like people to think his area has more crime than other areas."

However, Downey told *The Daily News* he wanted to see the breakdown and hoped the police department would release the statistics. He also said he didn't think crime on Gottingen Street was worse than it is in other parts of the city.

In an attempt at damage control, HPD Deputy Chief Dave MacKinnon said politics has nothing to do with the department's policy of refusing to release area breakdowns of crime statistics. "Statistics can be very deceiving," MacKinnon told *The Daily News*.

Truer words were never spoken. The old saying about "lies, damned lies and statistics" is more than just a cliché. And the issue of crime and policing in the Gottingen Street area involves more than just statistics.

What it involves is a tap-dance around a potentially explosive issue: race.

The release of race and crime statistics has become an object of heated debate, not only in Nova Scotia but also in other parts of Canada. Blacks aren't the only race involved in that debate. In Vancouver, Chinese-Canadians have protested crime statistics with as much vehemence as Jamaican-Canadians have in Toronto. Native Canadians are also angry over similar statistics in Manitoba.

Whatever the color involved, minority groups' common complaint is that misuse of crime statistics perpetuates stereotypes and provides unnecessary ammunition to the white-supremacist fringe. They also fail to take into account other variables such as the effects of poverty and racial discrimination.

Because the Gottingen Street area has a large black population, any matter affecting it almost automatically becomes a race issue. And any report that shows blacks being arrested and convicted in disproportionately high numbers will trigger instant and vehement protest from the community — or, at least, its media-friendly leaders.

This is the "politics" and "controversy" to which police officials alluded in *The Herald* pieces. An unidentified officer made it very plain when he said: "If there's a problem in the black community, the black community is the one right now that's making the most political waves. Because of that, you're getting upper management and politicians who don't want to hear 'the police did this to me because I'm black.'"

The officer went on to imply that police are reluctant to enforce the law in black areas like Gottingen Street because department officials will leave them twisting in the breeze if charges of racism arise.

If these attitudes are as pervasive as the officer makes them out to be, then there's trouble ahead for both the Gottingen Street area and the police department. Relations between the two can only become worse unless something's done soon.

The real victims of this dilemma are the law-abiding black people who are swimming against the tide of a system that is stacked against them. On the one hand, they are preyed upon by the criminal element within their community; on the other they are harassed by certain police officers who think all blacks look alike and must by definition be guilty of something. Talk about being caught between a rock and a hard place ....

There's a crying need for hard work and education on both sides. Although there is plenty of evidence of racism on the part of some police officers, the black community should also remember that some of our people who get arrested really are criminals and really do need to be put behind bars. The community knows the difference between the bad actors and the innocent victims; it's up to the police to learn that difference as well.

Black youths should never be allowed to believe they can get away with anything simply by yelling "Racism!" when they get caught. But they should also be taught to recognize and resist racism when they see it.

Police departments — not only in Halifax, but also in other parts of the province — need to bite the bullet, get rid of officers and administrators who harbor racist attitudes, and replace them with people who possess knowledge and understanding of the black community. HPD's recent minority recruitment drive is a step in the right direction, although one doesn't necessarily have to be black to learn to understand the community.

Only then will law-abiding blacks trust the police in the same way that law-abiding whites do. Maybe then, the windows of the Charlie Zone office will remain unbroken.

Set-asides:
County response a disgrace
March 14, 1993

Halifax County Council's recent decision to turn down a proposal for a panel to monitor set-asides of projects for local black businesses represents a major setback in race relations. And even if race were not an issue, the outcome of the vote would still be at best misguided, and at worst disgraceful.

By a 6-4 vote, the council's executive committee rejected an idea that would have improved the set-aside program's image in the wake of controversy over a contract that was not completed. Now, there's nothing left but rancor. It appears that ingrained patterns of belief and behavior are highly resistant to change.

The original purpose of the set-aside program was to give black contractors in Halifax County a chance to gain enough work experience to make competitive bids in the open market. Over the years, some black firms in the area were able to make inroads into the contracting business, but far too many others could not overcome barriers of racial bias. The set-asides were put in place to break some of those barriers, not to promote a reverse form of racism, as some critics complained.

By any rational standard, the nearly two-year-old program has been a resounding success. According to Beverley Clahane, chairwoman of the set-aside committee, only two out of 19 contracts awarded to black businesses led to difficulties. Seventeen-for-19 is an excellent batting average in any league.

However, rationality and race have seldom proved to be comfortable bedfellows. In terms of the racial thinking that has been prevalent over the past few centuries, one black failure automatically negates 10, 100, 1,000 black successes. And in the case of the set-asides, one of the two problem contracts happened to be the largest awarded — over $300,000 to Colonel Construction for a water project in Cherry Brook.

Colonel encountered problems paying some of its subcontractors, and the county picked up the tab for $88,000 in unpaid bills. Another black firm completed the water project.

In the wake of the Colonel case, the county suspended all set-asides early last January. That decision was both intemperate and prejudicial.

76

The source of the problem was Colonel Construction, not the entire black business community.

After strenuous objections from the Black Business Consortium and the Black United Front, Halifax County Council reinstated the set-aside program. There was, however, talk of placing limits on the amount of money an individual company could receive. To avoid any repetition of the problem with Colonel Construction, no more large contracts would be awarded.

It was the same old story: if one black person messes up, the entire race is held accountable.

That was the bad news. The good news was that the program would continue. As well, Halifax County Mayor Laszlo Lichter recommended the establishment of a watchdog panel to monitor and provide advice on future set-asides. The proposed panel would have included representatives from the black community.

Lichter suggested BUF, the Black Business Consortium, and the Watershed Associated Development Enterprises as sources for membership on the panel. County council would also have been represented. Although the panel was conceived through an overreaction to the Colonel Construction problem, it would have allowed blacks more input into the set-aside process.

Earlier this month, however, the idea encountered criticism from Councillor Ron Cooper, who suggested that black representatives on the panel might use their position to steer business their own way. "Self-interest" was the term Cooper used. Of course, he had no evidence to support his speculations.

This unfounded insinuation of potential dishonesty on the part of blacks was outrageous, to say the least. It insulted potential black members of the panel; it insulted the black businesspeople of Halifax County; and it insulted the black community as a whole. If Cooper had advanced such implications about anyone else, he would have been hung out to dry.

But he wasn't talking about anyone else; he was talking about blacks. And council agreed to refer the question of the watchdog panel to the executive committee for "further study."

In the meantime another councillor, Harry McInroy, reinforced Cooper's misgivings. Instead of rejecting those groundless notions out of hand, council's executive committee caved in and voted 6-4 against the formation of the watchdog panel.

The message of that vote to the black community is loud and clear: "We don't trust you."

And that lack of trust is based on the flimsy foundation of two failed set-asides out of 19 and the say-so of two reactionary county councillors.

Time out:
Swing anti-pimp bat at right targets
May 16, 1993

A loud sigh of relief must have resounded through the sordid spots of Canada last month upon the publication in *The Globe and Mail* of the following words from Deborah Jones's article, entitled Skirmishes In The Skin Trade: "When Joan is out on the baseball mound, the ball spinning toward her, she likes to imagine she's about to swing her bat at the head of a black pimp."

The sigh of relief would have come from all the non-black pimps who now realize that their heads are safe from the vengeful arc of "Joan's" baseball bat.

"Joan," a Halifax resident, is the pseudonymous subject of Jones's feature on the current crackdown against a nation-wide pimping ring. Most of the men arrested over the past several months have been black, with roots in North Preston. Sickening details of kidnappings, intimidation and assaults with a variety of weapons against under-age girls forced into the sex-for-sale business have emerged during high-profile pimping trials in Toronto and Halifax.

"Joan's" anger is understandable. Her under-age daughter became involved in the prostitution business, much to the mother's despair. Although "Joan" acknowledges problems in the home, this is how she describes her daughter's voluntary initiation into prostitution: "She's brazen, she figures she can take care of herself. She started hanging around with black kids. That's not meant to be a prejudiced remark. It's all black guys they (prostitutes) end up with, all from North Preston. Initially, her friends were not pimps, but were friends of pimps."

"Joan" may not have meant her comments to be prejudicial. But that's what they are, in more ways than one.

Is it true that only "brazen" white girls "hang around" with black kids? Is being the friend of a pimp the same thing as actually being a pimp? Is the simple act of befriending blacks the first step on a short road to perdition?

It is comments like "Joan's" that have caused North Preston to retreat behind a wall of media silence and the Nova Scotian black community as a whole to react defensively concerning the issue, saying, for example, that the police appear to be singling blacks out as targets in the anti-pimping campaign. (A few weeks ago, an adult white male was arrested on pimping charges — the first in over 30 such arrests in metro. A white young offender and two women have also been charged.)

This defensiveness is often mistaken as an exercise in denial and excuse-making. Not so. Speaking out against invidious stereotypes is one thing; condoning the beating of helpless women with heated coat hangers is something altogether different. No responsible person in the black community approves the kind of behavior that has been attributed to the pimping suspects. And, contrary to some opinions, there are plenty of responsible citizens in the black community. There are plenty of responsible citizens in North Preston.

But even responsible people can become sick to death of being made scapegoats for a problem that extends well beyond their geographical and racial borders. Breaking up a pimping ring is the job of the police; breaking down a community's reputation is the job of racists.

People who are involved in the prostitution business deserve to be punished under the law. Soliciting sex for hire is still illegal in this country, the pipe dreams of social reformers who want to legalize "red-light districts" notwithstanding.

But we should take our baseball bats of moral outrage and swing them at the conditions that create the sex trade as it exists today.

Let's swing our bats at the economic, educational and discriminatory conditions that exist in black communities. A disproportionate number of young black men may be choosing to become pimps, but these men also face a disproportionately narrow range of alternatives. If the range of alternatives in Nova Scotia widens, the number of pimps from the black community will drop. That's not an excuse; it's an explanation.

Let's swing our bats at familial and household breakdowns that cause young girls of all colors to leave their homes and become vulnerable to the lure of street life. Not every teen prostitute is kidnapped or coerced into the business. Some have said they would rather stay on the streets than return home.

Let's swing our bats at the forgotten factor in the prostitution equation: the customers. In *The Globe and Mail* article, Jones wrote: "... as a rule, police forces have chosen not to actively discourage the men who buy sex." Well, why not? Isn't the act of paying to have sexual intercourse with an under-age girl a clear-cut case of child molestation? Isn't a person who would do such a thing just as reprehensible as the one who puts that same girl out to work the streets?

Finally, let's swing our bats at the racist stereotypes that lead to bitterness and alienation among blacks. Maybe then we'll be able to fight decisive battles against the skin trade, as opposed to mere skirmishes.

RCMP snooping no surprise
April 17, 1994

Shock. Outrage. Those are the words most frequently heard in reaction to last week's revelation that the RCMP had spied on Nova Scotia's civil rights advocates during the late 1960s and early '70s. One of those advocates was Burnley "Rocky" Jones, who has since become a lawyer, and his ex-wife Joan, who writes columns for *The Herald*. Ironically, Rocky Jones' family is featured in *Hymn to Freedom*, a four-part TV documentary on black Canadian history.

Documents obtained by the Canadian Press under the Access to Information Act revealed that the RCMP was concerned that the Black Panther Party, a militant U.S. organization, was planning on inciting the "normally docile colored population" of Nova Scotia to violence. Panther party members had visited Halifax in November of 1968, and local police arrested one Panther, George Sams, Jr., on gun-possession charges.

The documents also indicated that the RCMP snoopers harbored vicious racial stereotypes about blacks, particularly those in Nova Scotia's historically black communities. Black women were called "prolific child bearers"; men were considered drunks and thieves who worked only sporadically; Panther recruits were "illiterate, semi-illiterate, and hoodlums."

The anger generated by both the spying — which extended to entire black communities and organizations and even dance clubs — and the perpetuation of blatantly bigoted stereotypes is understandable. The Nova Scotia legislature has denounced the spying, and rightly so.

Reactions of shock and surprise, on the other hand, seem somewhat naive.

Racial stereotypes of the sort expressed by the RCMP's sleuths have existed for hundreds of years, and promise to continue well into the next century. The investigators obviously went into the black communities with preconceived notions, then proceeded to see what they wanted to see and hear what they wanted to hear to confirm their prejudices.

That's hardly surprising.

Even less surprising is the fear the prospect of Black Panther "infiltration" provoked. Today, the Panthers are at best a fading memory. However, for a five-year period from 1967 to 1972, the Black Panthers were the most feared radical group in the U.S. Some of that fear spilled across the border to Canada.

With their black leather jackets and berets, open defiance of police and other authorities, advocacy of armed rebellion against racism, and charismatic leaders like Huey Newton and Eldridge Cleaver, the Panthers were a nightmare to such defenders of the status quo as the FBI in the U.S. and the RCMP in Canada.

The FBI and local police forces declared war on the Panthers, and the party eventually perished as its members came out on the losing end of shootouts and ambushes. Newton was jailed, and later died in a drug-related shooting. Cleaver fled to Cuba and Algeria, then returned to the U.S. as a born-again Christian. Ultimately, the Panthers became victims of the violence they promoted.

In Canada, the Panthers never established a lasting presence. Yet the RCMP considered the party the spark that could ignite an "explosive situation" in the black communities of Nova Scotia.

William Higgitt, the RCMP's main spy, wrote in December 1968: "U.S. Black Panther members have been actively engaged in attempts to gain control of the civil-rights leadership in the Halifax and area Negro community."

His evidence for that conclusion was the presence of a Panther — T.D. Pawley — at a major black community meeting held at the North Branch Library earlier that month. That meeting marked the birth of the Black United Front.

There were, however, no further visits from the Panthers, and no chapter of the party ever formed in Nova Scotia.

The RCMP's behavior at that time was typical rather than surprising. Instead of contributing to the amelioration of the poverty and discrimination at the root of the "explosive situation" in the black communities, the authorities chose to chase an external threat that existed mostly in their own minds.

Report on black learners adds to history
February 19, 1995

When the Black Learners Advisory Committee released its three-volume report, *Redressing Inequity — Empowering Black Learners*, last December, a major chapter was added to the history of blacks in this province.

Ask most people to think of two words that explain the problems of blacks in Nova Scotia, and the answers you'd get are likely to be "racism" and "education" — too much of the former and too little of the latter.

BLAC's report documents the history of two sorry centuries of segregated education; analyzes how that history has continued to affect black learners through three decades of integration; and advances recommendations geared toward transforming the difficulties of the past and present into a promising future.

It was the report's recommendations — 46 in all — that raised ripples of controversy at the end of 1994. The bones of contention included:

The creation of scholarships to bring 200 new black teachers during the next 10 years to help redress the under-representation of black teachers in the public education system;

Funding of anti-racism initiatives for all 22 of the province's school boards;

Establishment of an Afrocentric Learning Institute to give black children "the opportunity to experience an appropriate cultural education which gives them an intimate knowledge of, and which honors and respects, the history and culture of black people."

For some critics, the latter recommendation raised the spectre of resegregation, of relegating black students into an academic ghetto. Those critics fail to understand that "Afrocentric" learning would be in addition to, not instead of, the core curriculum all students would receive. Also, such a measure would be temporary, lasting only until integration is achieved in both the curriculum and the classroom.

In the best of worlds, implementation of BLAC's recommendations would already be underway. However, in the real world, which is far from the best, the report is being studied by the Department of Education.

The report — especially the second volume, which reviews the history of black education in the province — should be read by all Nova Scotians, not just education department functionaries.

Most of the report's material concerning 19th- and early 20th-century educational racism can be found in other sources such as Bridglal Pachai's *Beneath the Clouds of the Promised Land* and James Walker's *A History of Blacks in Canada: A Study Guide for Teachers and Students*.

But the BLAC's research has also found some fascinating new information from the past 50 years. This information is presented in "case studies" focusing on the academic experiences of people in Inglewood, a small Nova Scotian black community, and North Preston. There are also case studies on two of the province's best-known educational initiatives: the Black Incentive Fund, and Dalhousie University's Transition Year Program.

Among the case studies' gems:

Inglewood, which is located near Bridgetown in the Annapolis Valley and never had a population numbering more than 100, managed to graduate as many as 95 per cent of its students from Grade 12 after the area's schools were integrated. Despite this record of excellence, however, "to this present day (1994), Bridgetown has yet to hire their first black teacher."

North Preston's strife with the school system was dramatized during the fights at Cole Harbour High School in 1989 and last year's feud with white parents at the Ross Road School.

Redressing Inequity shows that the battle has been going on for nearly two centuries. At one point in the late 19th century, North Preston had gone without a school for 15 years. The community has done everything from hiring an African-American educator, Frisell Jones, in the 1950s to launching a class-action suit in the 1970s. Yet the area continues to be plagued by high dropout rates.

The report condemns the Black Incentive Fund as a well-intended initiative that has "failed to meet its stated objectives." Before its radical overhaul at the beginning of the 1990s, the fund achieved notoriety as a program that "paid black students to go to school." Despite that stigma, BLAC recommends that the fund be retained in the role of an incentive for access to universities and other post-secondary institutes.

Although the Transition Year Program, which provides a post-secondary opportunity for Nova Scotian blacks and Mi'kmaq, has existed for 25 years, much of that existence has been spent on a shaky tightrope. More than once, the program has faced oblivion. Recently, however, Dalhousie University made a 10-year committment to keep TYP going, and the program's first black Nova Scotian director, Beverly Johnson, was hired. For all TYP's troubles, the report says the program is "as much needed today as it was 20 years ago because the public system has not changed significantly."

Perhaps all the recommendations in *Redressing Inequity* will be enacted some day. Then again, in the current era of government fiscal austerity, maybe none of them will. But regardless of the political outcome, BLAC has produced a document of enduring historical significance. For that reason alone, the report is well worth the time and money involved in its production.

A setback for North Preston
May 19, 1996

North Preston is a community beset by stereotypes. For nearly all its history, which encompasses more than 200 years, the residents of Canada's oldest and largest black community have struggled against poverty, neglect, racism and a negative media image. Sometimes they win that struggle. And sometimes they lose.

But it wasn't stereotypes that pelted RCMP and Halifax Regional Police vehicles with a barrage of rocks last Monday night. It wasn't stereotypes that trapped three outsiders in a house in the community. It wasn't stereotypes that prevented the police from leaving the area until reinforcements were called in.

No, it was real people. People who should have known better. People who may have done irreparable harm to their community.

By now, the events of last Monday are familiar to news-watchers across Canada. Four young black men from Toronto — three Jamaican-Canadians and one North Preston native — were involved in a car crash in New Brunswick. In the aftermath, a large sum of money — $3,000 — went missing after the men were separated.

The North Preston man, Darrell Downey, went to his home town. The Jamaicans followed him there and asked him where the money was. Dissatisfied with Downey's answer, they roughed him up. They were, in turn, intimidated by other members of the community and fled to another house.

A crowd gathered and confined the Jamaicans to the house. They called the police. The RCMP arrived, but the crowd, which numbered in the hundreds, would not allow them to leave with the three Jamaicans.

Hours of negotiations ensued, and more police arrived. The police again attempted to leave with the outsiders, and were again blocked. Reporters and photographers who had come to the scene were threatened by some in the crowd. Finally, late that night, the Jamaicans were taken out of North Preston by a convoy of police vehicles.

And then all hell broke loose. A segment of the crowd lined up on both sides of the street unleashed a torrent of rocks at the cars, smashing windows and windshields. Broken glass injured eight officers, and the overall cost of the incident was estimated at $150,000 or more.

It was images of the rock-throwing and its aftermath that lit up TV screens throughout Canada last week. The scene was reminiscent of Chatauguay, Quebec in 1990, when a mob of angry whites stoned a convoy of natives at the height of the Oka crisis.

In other adverse circumstances over the years, North Preston has received the short end of the stick in its encounters with police, the media and the municipal government. In the Cole Harbour High School brawls of 1989, only blacks were convicted even though both blacks and whites participated in the fights. The crackdown on pimps during the early 1990s focused unfairly on North Preston. And the late, unlamented East Lake landfill would have placed a noxious facility too close to the community.

But this time, there are no mitigating factors. Yes, relations between the police and the Preston area are not what they should be. Blacks complain justifiably about being followed, stopped and suspected simply because they are black.

However, those complaints don't apply in this case. The police weren't harassing anyone last Monday; they were trying to prevent what might have turned into a disaster. Once the police took the three Jamaicans into custody, there was no reason to block their exit from the community.

Indeed, the police displayed admirable restraint. They could have responded with gunfire as they ran the gauntlet of rock-throwers. They could have returned in force and arrested half the community. Instead, they are proceeding slowly — perhaps too slowly for those who prefer swift justice and swifter punishment.

One hero did emerge from this tragedy — Viola Cain, the woman who sheltered the three Jamaicans during the lengthy standoff.

Some of the people whose faces appeared on national TV complained bitterly about the way North Preston is covered in the media. They said only the bad things about the community ever make it into the news, never the good.

Ironically, Cain, who is raising five foster children, had been profiled only weeks before in a "good news" story in *The Herald*. A similar story appeared in *Black Focus* magazine.

Cain's role in the standoff has been downplayed. And some members of the community have criticized her for giving refuge to the outsiders. But if Cain hadn't given them sanctuary and had left them to the mercy of the mob, it is highly likely a near-tragedy would have turned into a catastrophe from which North Preston might never have recovered. Her critics ought to be grateful for her courage and good judgment.

Cain symbolizes the good side of North Preston. There are many others like her in the community — church choir leaders, paving contractors, civil servants, mechanics, day-care workers. Quietly and with far less fanfare than they deserve, the Viola Cains struggle to build up what the rock-throwers are tearing down.

The people of North Preston need to apologize to the police and offer to make restitution for the damage caused in the melee. And they need to repudiate the rock-throwers.

They need to do this not to restore their reputation outside their area, but to reaffirm the integrity that has enabled the community to survive privations that would have broken anyone else.

Otherwise, the stereotypes will become reality.

A comeback from a setback
June 2, 1996

For every action, there is an equal and opposite reaction. That's a law of physics. Its equivalent law in human society is this: for every unsettling event that occurs, there is an equally disruptive backlash.

This action-reaction sequence is especially prevalent in race relations. Events that involve the black community in some negative way are usually followed by an equally negative backlash from whites.

If that pattern proved true in every case, this column would be about a backlash caused by the May 13 melee in North Preston. Eight RCMP officers were injured and 20 vehicles damaged when a group of people in the community stoned a police convoy that escorted three outsiders involved in a dispute over $3,000 who had been trapped by an angry crowd. Images of the disturbance appeared in print and electronic media across Canada.

Ordinarily, an event such as this would have sparked a backlash that would have continued for several weeks, if not months. But this time, the negative reaction only lasted a day, if that long.

On the day after the melee, the RCMP took a hard line, promising charges and arrests for what Superintendent Lorne Hall called a "reprehensible act." That indignation was understandable, considering the potential injury the officers faced under a volley of brick-sized rocks.

However, the ire of the police was offset by the gratitude some North Preston residents expressed for the way the incident was handled. Their restraint in the face of violence received a great deal of praise.

Later in the week, it appeared that police officers may have been as upset with each other as they were with the rock-throwers. Some Halifax regional police officers who had also been called to the scene accused the RCMP of poor communications and using the regional officers as a "decoy" while the RCMP escorted the three outsiders to safety. Police from both branches later met to resolve their differences.

Notably absent from the immediate reaction to the events were anti-community comments from the police, and anti-police comments from the community.

Letters to the editor and call-in shows often serve as a backlash barometer, as does *The Daily News* Hotline. Other violent or criminal events involving black people in general and people from North Preston in particular tend to precipitate a flood of racist responses.

Not this time, though. Hardly any letters about the incident appeared in either *The Daily News* or *The Herald* newspapers. The majority of Hotline callers thought the police had handled the situation well. Some thought North Preston was to blame and suggested that a special tax be imposed on the community to recover the estimated $150,000 in damage and police overtime costs. However, the usual racist ranting this type of Hotline question sets off was absent.

Theo Moudakis' cartoon showing a young black man saying "Well, we already had the mob together ... so we figured ... may as well go after the cops and the press ..." received some criticism, notably from a young black woman and the inspector of the Cole Harbour RCMP detachment. But it should be clear that the face in the cartoon was meant to represent only the people who participated in the rock-throwing, not North Preston or the black community as a whole.

So far, the response of the police and public in the aftermath of the incident has been subdued. Reflections on what might have happened on May 13 — even more serious injuries and possible deaths — may have had a greater effect than the actual events, traumatic as they were.

To date, five people have been arrested in connection with the melee on charges ranging from assault on a police officer to "obstruction." Bail for some of the "obstruction" charges has been set at $15,000. That appears to be an excessive amount, considering that in a drug-trafficking case earlier this year, bail for four suspects was $1,000 each.

However, the true fly in the ointment has been columnist Harry Flemming. I agreed with part of the message he conveyed in his musings last week. Yes, the media concentrates on "bad news" and "man bites dog" stories, primarily because that's the kind of news readers, watchers and listeners desire, their protestations to the contrary notwithstanding.

And yes, people from North Preston need to take some responsibility for their own behavior, as do people from every other community.

But Flemming couldn't stop there. Having made his obvious points, he then, in all his patronizing pomposity, slurred North Preston as being "somewhat overgiven to crime." And he launched a totally uncalled-for attack on Preston MLA and Environment Minister Wayne Adams for trying to "mitigate the crime by citing media provocation" in his nationally televised comments on the melee.

Adams did no such thing. He merely pointed out Preston residents' perceptions about how they are depicted in media reports. To claim that means Adams was attempting to "mitigate the crime" is a stretch, to say the least.

Fortunately, Flemming's bile didn't spill over to last month's official opening of the RCMP's community-policing office at the Black Cultural Centre. Despite the intensity of the May 13 incident, a report described the atmosphere at the opening as "jovial."

RCMP Constable Gary MacConnell is the community-policing officer stationed at the new facility. He was also injured in the *mêlée*, and had to have glass slivers plucked from the cornea of his eye. At the opening ceremony, he said of the incident: "I think both community and police have learned from this and it may have been a blessing in disguise."

It's a hell of a disguise. But maybe MacConnell's words will prove prophetic. The old, sadly predictable pattern of race relations in Metro has been broken this time. It's up to everyone — the community, the police and the media — to ensure that it stays broken.

Dal's Minority Law Program goes under the microscope
August 3, 1997

A furor has erupted over Dalhousie Law School's Indigenous Black and Mi'kmaq program. Last week, a review committee's report said graduates from the IBM program are having difficulty finding jobs in local law firms. The report also suggested that standards of admission for IBM students are lower than those for other students accepted into the law school, and their performance in the classroom is poorer. As well, the report says IBM students feel "segregated" in their relations with other students.

At this point, it should be mentioned that IBM students take the same courses as everyone else, and they must pass the same bar examination to become lawyers. IBM is not a separate course of studies; it's an admissions and support program.

Publication of the report's findings in the media has upset some students and faculty, including IBM director Carol Aylward. Aylward argues that the negative aspects of the report will create even greater difficulties for IBM graduates. She also says only eight IBM students have flunked out since the program's inception in 1989.

Sad to say, Aylward is probably right about the fallout from the report.

But the designers of the program should have seen this train coming. They should have realized misperceptions about the program and its students would be inevitable. They should have had measures in place to contradict those misperceptions. The IBM program's successes ought to be receiving at least as much publicity as its difficulties.

The program started in response to a recommendation from the Donald Marshall wrongful-imprisonment inquiry. The commission said more Mi'kmaq and blacks should be included in Nova Scotia's legal system. That way, the system would be more reflective of, and responsible to, the entire population of the province.

Progress has been made in that regard. Nova Scotia now has two black judges. There are black lawyers at both prosecution and defence tables in the courtrooms. IBM graduates have set up private practices.

Still, the committee's report indicated that none of the IBM students who articled — a form of post-graduate apprenticeship — with law firms in this province has been hired full-time.

There may well be a glut of new lawyers in the system. But a nine-year snub of IBM graduates is unconscionable.

If IBM graduates are slamming into a stone wall (never mind a glass ceiling) in their attempts to get jobs in their field after graduation, something is seriously wrong.

Are the doubts about IBM students' ability and qualifications harbored by certain faculty and students at Dal's law school echoed in Nova Scotia's law firms?

Undoubtedly, they are. But the inevitable existence of such doubts is a price all affirmative-action programs must pay. It should be emphasized here that affirmative-action programs do not create race-related doubts or perceptions of inferiority. They simply give people another excuse to express the racist views they've always held, and would continue to hold even if all affirmative-action programs were abolished tomorrow.

Is the bitter coinage of doubts and intimations of inferiority exacted from a program like Dal's IBM a price worth paying?

Yes — if in the long run its graduates get the opportunity to demonstrate their ability, to disprove doubts, to open the door for other minority-group members and, ultimately, to end the need for affirmative-action programs.

But if IBM graduates can't even get in on the ground floor of the legal system, then it's time for the program to do some rethinking.

It's also time for the Nova Scotia law establishment to take a hard look at its attitudes. The Marshall Commission report said the establishment is part of the problem minorities have with the system, and suggested how it could become part of the solution. Shutting out IBM graduates is not part of the solution.

As for the "segregation" problem at the law school — eventually, these students will be working together as officers of the court. They had better learn how to get along while they're in school, because they're not going to be working in separate legal systems after they graduate.

Justice for Judge Corrine Sparks
October 5, 1997

During the last week of September, blacks south of the border commemorated the 40th anniversary of the traumatic integration of Central High School in Little Rock, Arkansas.

The day after that celebration, blacks in Nova Scotia also took a step into history.

On Friday, September 26, the Supreme Court of Canada reinstated Family Court Judge Corrine Sparks's acquittal of a black youth who had been charged with assaulting a white police officer and resisting arrest. Because of remarks Sparks had made about the racial context of the case, her decision was overturned by the Nova Scotia Supreme Court and a new trial was ordered. The Nova Scotia Court of Appeal upheld that ruling. The youth, represented by lawyer Burnley "Rocky" Jones, then appealed his case to the highest court in the land.

And, by a 6-to-3 decision, the Supreme Court of Canada has upheld Sparks' original not-guilty verdict.

The incident that led to the youth's arrest was a he-said-he-said situation. The police officer, Constable Donald Steinburg, was arresting a black youth on suspicion of car theft when another black youth, aged 15 at the time, approached on a bicycle. From that point, the stories diverge.

According to Steinburg, the youth ran his bike into him and raised his voice, prompting Steinburg to arrest him. The youth said he was talking to his peer and was told to shut up or he would be arrested.

The officer and the youth were the only witnesses in Sparks's court. Ordinarily, in that kind of circumstance, it's case closed. The judge believes the cop, and the defendant is found guilty.

Not this time, though.

Having worked within the legal system as a lawyer and judge, Sparks would have understood where Steinburg was coming from. And as a black Nova Scotian, she understood where the youth was coming from. She weighed those two parts of her life experience along with the evidence, and acquitted the youth. And some of the words she used in her decision precipitated a legal firestorm.

Those words, which have been continually repeated and will probably appear in the law books of the future, are: "I'm not saying that the constable has misled the court, although police officers have been known to do that in the past. And I'm not saying the officer over-reacted, but certainly police officers do over-react, particularly when they are dealing with non-white groups."

On the basis of those words, the decision was appealed and over-turned. In the higher courts and the media, Sparks was accused of having a pro-black, anti-police bias. Only one judge, Justice Gerald Freeman of the Nova Scotia Appeal Court, supported Sparks. In his dissent from the appeal court's ruling, Freeman said: "The case was racially charged, a classic confrontation between a white police officer representing the power of the state and a black youth charged with an offence.

"Judge Sparks was under a duty to be sensitive to the nuances and implications, and to rely on her own common sense, which is generally informed by her own experience and understanding.

"It is unfortunately true and within the scope of general knowledge of any individual that police officers have been known to mislead the court and over-react in dealing with non-white groups."

Six of the nine Supreme Court of Canada judges agreed with Free-man. In part, their opinion stated: "As a member of the community, it was open to (Sparks) to take into account the well-known presence of racism in that community, and to evaluate the evidence as to what occurred against that background."

The dissenting trio thought race wasn't the issue in the case, and Sparks should not have made it an issue in her ruling.

Their sharp disagreement with the majority reflects the racial divisions that exist in Nova Scotia and other parts of North America in which people of African and European descent attempt to co-exist.

There are several winners in this outcome.

Obviously, the youth who was willing to go to the highest court to seek justice is a winner. He proved that persistence pays, and his victory is partial compensation for the reverses blacks have suffered in the court system in the past.

Sparks is also a clear winner. Her judgement has been vindicated at the highest level, and those who pilloried her alleged "bias" are now wiping egg off their faces.

Rocky Jones is a winner. As a so-called "dangerous radical," he was spied upon by the RCMP during the 1960s and '70s. He joined the legal system at a late age, and within a few months of passing his bar examination he has argued and won a Supreme Court case.

Dalhousie Law School's Indigenous Black and Mi'kmaq program is a winner. Jones obtained access to law school through the IBM program. His success at the Supreme Court level should shut the mouths of those who say IBM students lack qualifications to become lawyers.

Is there a loser? Yes — racism.

In the late 1990s, it has become fashionable to pretend racism doesn't exist and disparage those who insist it does. Hopefully, the Supreme Court's decision will provide a much-needed wake-up call for the nay-sayers.

Are the police losers? Only if they want to be.

Too far, too fast
November 2, 1997

What do you do when you're turned down at the top? That's what the family of Warren Edward Sheppard, Jr. must decide now that Premier Russell MacLellan has turned down their request for a provincial inquiry into the circumstances of Sheppard's death.

Eddie Sheppard was stabbed to death on March 13, 1996, by Albert Ian MacDonald, his housemate at a small-options home for former mental health patients. MacDonald was tried and found not guilty by reason of insanity, and was sentenced to an indefinite stay in the forensic unit of the Nova Scotia Hospital.

The Sheppard family has been pressing the province for an inquiry to find out why MacDonald, who has a long record of violent behavior, was placed with Eddie, and to develop policies that would prevent other tragedies.

In a recent letter to family spokesman Raymond Sheppard, MacLellan says: "Mr. Sheppard's death occurred in a private facility. After a police investigation into his death, there was a subsequent involvement of the criminal justice system. The Department of Community Services has conducted a thorough program audit of the facility which housed Mr. Sheppard, and there has also been a systems-wide audit of all small-options homes in the province. The minister of justice was of the view that a public inquiry was not warranted in the circumstances of this case. As a result of the minister of justice's recommendation, I cannot direct that the minister of community services hold a public inquiry into the operations of small-options homes."

The Sheppards have been thwarted at the highest level of the provincial government. Where can they go from here?

"We want to save someone else from suffering the same fate that our brother succumbed to," says Raymond Sheppard. "So far, it's Murder 1, Eddie 0. We're not looking for special treatment here; we're looking for that which is just and that which is right. We want to continue to express to Nova Scotians that mental health matters."

Frustrated by fruitless efforts to gain government action, the Sheppards are ready to carry their case beyond the walls of Province House.

"We want to make the need for a inquiry a part of the next provincial election," Sheppard says. "We want mental health consumers in the province of Nova Scotia to have their voices heard. We want them to rally around the necessary changes so that mental health consumers can feel they have their rights protected by the government . . . or a government."

The Sheppards feel let down by the MacLellan government, not to mention the mental health system.

That system has undergone major transformations over the past 30 years. Because of advances in drug treatments for mental disorders, many people who would have undergone long stays in hospitals have been "de-institutionalized" — released into the community.

Unfortunately, little was done to prepare the community at large to accept the de-institutionalized. Good intentions gone awry have resulted in hopelessness, homelessness and death.

Sheppard believes his brother was in part the victim of a de-institutionalization process that has gone "too far, too fast." And he deplores the lack of support for people with mental health problems.

"If there's not the services, if there's not the programs in place to accommodate the people that are released from institutions, then they are put at a disadvantage," Sheppard says.

"Quite often, mentally challenged persons are abandoned by the social-services system. The system seems to lack human compassion when it comes to dealing with mental health consumers."

Race also matters. Although Sheppard is not certain race was a direct factor in his brother's death, he does believe the mental health establishment is as influenced by race as any other system in a race-conscious society. He believes the system responds differently to blacks than it does to whites.

"I feel that African-Nova Scotians do not reach out quite often for mental-health services because they are afraid of the system not responding to their special needs," Sheppard says.

"And there are very few mental health practitioners in Nova Scotia that they can identify with, because there are very few black psychologists or other mental-health workers. The system does not reflect us; therefore, how can it treat us? The diversity is not there at all."

Sheppard also thinks race was a factor in the province's refusal to hold an inquiry into his brother's death. "When you look into the inquiries in Nova Scotia that have been held over the last 20 years, with the exception of the Donald Marshall inquiry, 99 per cent have been based on Anglo-Saxon Caucasians as opposed to any inquiries based on African-Canadian needs or requirements."

Now, the Sheppards are asking the public for help, not only to get to the bottom of Eddie's death, but also to bring mental-health issues out of the shadows of dismissal and denial, and to remove the stigma attached to mental health consumers.

"During the next provincial election, people have to let their MLAs know that they have concerns regarding this, and make it an election issue," Sheppard says. "It has to become an issue because for far too long, people have been at a disadvantage. Unless they have some way of venting their concerns, and making real changes, they are going to continue to be dumped upon, to the detriment of the greater society."

But the greater society has to become aware of the nature of that detriment, and what can be done to prevent it from becoming worse than it is. To that end, the Sheppards continue their labor of love. "Our efforts will not bring Eddie back," Sheppard says. "But that is not the reason we continue to strive. Our quest is to save someone else from suffering such a fate. If we can save one person from going to an untimely death because of the system, then we have served Eddie, and we have served to make Eddie's life worthwhile."

Carver Union shouldn't be discredited by bureaucracy
May 3, 1998

"It's very sad. It is one of the last remaining institutions that belongs to the black community . . . and they're picking us off one by one."

That was how Gus Wedderburn, president of the George Washington Carver Credit Union, described the recent closing of the East Preston-based institution. The union, Canada's only black-run financial institution, began back in 1950 because it was — and sometimes still is — difficult for blacks to obtain loans and credit from banks.

The late Noel Johnston of East Preston was the mainstay of the union until his death in late 1995. During the past two years, the institution struggled for survival. It was near death almost a year ago, when the province's Credit Union Deposit Insurance Corporation imposed a target of $400,000 as the union's deposit base.

June 30, 1997 was the deadline to reach that figure. When the union didn't reach the target amount by then, the deadline was extended. But the deposit level rose no higher than $350,000, despite fund-raising efforts that included the raffle of a Mercedes. So CUDIC finally ended the Carver Union's 48-year history of providing small loans to the Preston community.

Because the deposits were insured, the 503 members of the union got their money back. Wedderburn has voiced hopes the union could be revived. But it would have to be able to offer services such as cheque-writing, RRSPs and use of automatic-teller machines. To do so, it would have to raise $600,000 to $700,000 — twice the amount it had on hand at its dissolution.

Barry Bennett, CEO of the insurance corporation, said more community support might have saved the Carver Union. That's support from the black and non-black communities, as the union never closed its doors to non-black depositors.

Still, as Wedderburn said, the Carver Union "belonged" to the black community. And the black community let it go.

The last major black organization to fall by the wayside was the Black United Front, which was disbanded two years ago after nearly 30 years of advocating black Nova Scotian social and political causes. Although BUF did good work, the organization was plagued by internal divisions and became dependent on provincial funding for its survival. When the province withdrew that funding, BUF collapsed. Again, the black community let it go.

Wedderburn says "They're picking us off one by one." But could it be that the black community is abandoning its institutions, one by one?

BUF and the Carver Union are examples of institutions that could not muster enough community support to continue. Yet the demise of those two organizations doesn't necessarily constitute a negative trend.

Still, they can be seen as indicators of a transition in progress.

As in the rest of North America, Nova Scotia's black institutions were formed in the 1800s in response to segregation. Black churches have been around far longer than the Carver Union or BUF, as has the Nova Scotia Home for Colored Children.

With much effort, official segregation was ended. The circumstances under which black institutions operate thus changed. Their survival depends on how they adapt to those changes.

Because of their intimate ties to the communities they serve, the survival of Nova Scotia's black churches is guaranteed.

The Home for Colored Children survives because it opened its doors to non-black children and adapted to changing child-care philosophies.

If the Carver Union is to continue, it will probably need to follow the home's example: expand its services beyond the black community and adapt to new business realities. However, in the current age of mega-bank mergers, that may prove difficult.

Rosa Parks and the N-word
August 9, 1998

The more things change, the more they stay the same. That's one of the oldest clichés in the book. Yet time and time again, that old saying is proven to be true — especially when it comes to racial concerns.

A case in point occurred last week, when the celebrated civil-rights pioneer Rosa Parks came to Halifax to receive an honorary doctorate from Mount Saint Vincent University. Parks' refusal to surrender her seat on a Montgomery, Alabama bus to a white passenger back in 1955 is credited as the catalyst for a 10-year effort that ended legal segregation in the United States.

Her visit was a boost for Nova Scotia's black community. Almost all the publicity surrounding the event was positive. There was even a two-page feature on Parks and black Nova Scotians in the August 3 issue of *Maclean's* magazine.

But there was one negative incident — a reminder that the racism against which Parks and many others have battled has not been eradicated in the hearts and minds of all.

When Parks arrived at Halifax International Airport on Saturday, August 1, she was met by a crowd of more than 100 well-wishers, who greeted her with flowers and accolades.

At least one person at the airport, however, was not impressed.

As reported by Sue Coueslan in the next day's *Sunday Daily News*: "A tall man in the crowd with an American accent said with a chuckle: 'All this just for another old nigger.'"

That was a comment characteristic of "just another old bigot." It doesn't matter whether the speaker was old or young; the attitude he pungently expressed is as old as the dinosaurs, and ought to be just as extinct. This person's willingness to say something so offensive within earshot of others in the airport reflects a level of ignorance that is beyond redemption.

Obviously, his attitude was not shared by most of the other people who were at the airport, regardless of whether they had gone there to see Parks. Nor is it shared by most Nova Scotians; nor, for that matter, most Canadians and Americans.

Nor is it shared by Coueslan. Yet she, rather than the garbage-mouthed racist at the airport, has borne the brunt of the black community's anger over the incident and the way it was reported in *The Daily News*.

However, the man's comment was as offensive to Coueslan as it would be to anyone else who abhors his sentiments.

"There was an atmosphere of celebration at the airport," Coueslan recalls. "The people I was talking to were so proud that she was coming. They couldn't believe a person of such stature was here."

And Coueslan couldn't believe what she heard a few moments later.

"The RCMP were clearing the way for her (Parks), when this man made the comment. He was standing there, smiling and shaking his head when he made this comment. He just smiled. He wasn't the least bit ashamed of saying it. I was shocked."

The man later made similar remarks to *Daily News* photographer Mike Dembeck. "He said: 'They're nothing but trouble. You can keep 'em all,'" Dembeck recalls.

Coueslan had to decide whether or not to include the comment in her story about Parks's arrival. It was not an easy decision.

"I thought that guy doesn't deserve to have his comments put in the paper," she says. "On the other hand, the comment does reflect the fact that even 40 years after the incident with Rosa Parks on the bus, there's still all this work that needs to be done; that some people are still stupid and don't get it. So I made the decision to let the comment stay in."

When I first saw the comment in Coueslan's story, my reaction was anger — at the redneck who made it, not the writer who reported it. However, other members of the black community have expressed ire against Coueslan and *The Daily News* because they feel the comment detracted from what was otherwise a positive, even historic, event.

Given the negative reaction to the inclusion of the comment, Coueslan has had some second thoughts.

"I can't say I wish I didn't put it in," she says. "Because I still think that it does need to be addressed, and I stand behind why I decided it was the thing to do. I just wish it wasn't so misunderstood."

I can certainly understand the indignation other blacks have expressed over the incident. But it wasn't Coueslan or *The Daily News* that insulted Rosa Parks. It was a travelling racist who didn't have enough sense to keep his stupidity to himself. There's no discernible difference between him and the driver who ordered Parks to move to the back of the bus all those years ago.

And, unfortunately, there are still enough people like him around to ensure that the war Parks began when she stayed in her bus seat is not yet over. Many battles have been won since 1955, but some holdouts on the losing side still refuse to surrender.

Rosa Parks is 85 years old. During her lifetime, she has witnessed tremendous changes in the circumstances of blacks throughout the world. The legal segregation under which she grew up has been overturned, not just in the southern U.S. states, but also in northern states, and Canada, and South Africa. Opportunities in employment and education have opened. The number of black office-holders has burgeoned. The black middle class has grown and prospered. To say that nothing has changed for blacks during the second half of this century is to deny reality.

But to say that nothing remains the same is equally unrealistic. Racism continues to plague blacks and other minorities in ways that are large and small. It mutates like the HIV virus. Before, racism was simply the belief that whites are inherently superior to all other races. Now, it has morphed into the belief that minorities are being given unfair advantages over whites through affirmative-action programs. That is the racial battleground of the '90s, and will continue to be so well into the next century, at least until the next mutation occurs.

Laws can change. Policies can change. Times can change. But sometimes, attitudes stay set in stone — or, in the case of the airport commentator, the Stone Age.

So we should celebrate Rosa Parks, her courage, her dignity, and what she stands for. And we should not shoot the messenger who brings us news we'd rather not hear.

Johnnie Cochran — Advocate for justice
September 20, 1998

Johnnie L. Cochran Jr. came to Halifax last week to speak at a fund-raiser for Dalhousie University Law School's Indigenous Black and Mi'kmaq Program and Public Legal Education. He delivered a speech at the Rebecca Cohn Theatre, and later there was a $150-a-pop reception.

Earlier in the day, the Black Cultural Centre held an informal meet-and-greet session with Cochran. He didn't give a speech there; instead, he mingled with the blacks and whites who had come to see him, talking one-on-one or with small groups.

Cochran is a genuinely friendly man, and everyone who approached him received a smile, a handshake, and conversation.

The Air Canada strike played havoc with Cochran's original schedule, so he didn't have much time to be interviewed by the media. I was fortunate enough to be able to ask him two questions.

Of course, Cochran's name will always be associated with the acquittal of O.J. Simpson on double murder charges in 1995. Blacks and whites reacted in contrasting ways when a mostly black jury found the ex-football star not guilty of killing his former wife and her friend during the summer of 1994. Most blacks thought Simpson was being framed, and celebrated the verdict. On the other hand, most whites were convinced of Simpson's guilt, and were aghast at both the verdict and blacks' jubilant response.

So my first question to Cochran was: Do you think the fallout from the O.J. Simpson case has finally ended?

"I'd certainly like to think it's diminished," he said. "I'm not sure it's totally ended. The civil case is on appeal, and there are many people who say that under the laws of California for punitive damages, the intention is not to destroy, but just to punish. His net worth was estimated at $15 million. How is he supposed to pay $33 million? It doesn't make any sense. So if the courts follow the laws of California, that case will be reversed at some point, at least in terms of damages. If that happens, then you'll see real fallout, I'm sure."

My second question was broader in scope: What are the biggest problems facing black people today, and what can we do to solve them?

"I think the problems are similar in Nova Scotia and the United States," Cochran said. "There was a report released this March from the Eisenhower Foundation that basically took a look 30 years post-Kerner Commission, which was set up by President Lyndon Johnson after the riots in the cities. The commission came back and said we were moving toward two societies: one black, one white, both separate and unequal.

"The Eisenhower Foundation report, 30 years later, says we have now arrived at those two societies, one black, one white; they are separate and unequal. The major housing for the poor . . . has now become prison cells. Race and poverty are intertwined. They're pounding holes in the justice system.

"One in three young black males are either in prison, on parole, or on probation. Unemployment rates in the inner cities are astronomical. The stock-market surge has not impacted on African-American people.

"I think that we're going to have to, as we approach the new millennium, we as black people are going to have to structure our own agenda. We have to take responsibility for some of the things in our own community. We have to become advocates again for those things that are right.

"For instance, there are people in the United States who want to make the words 'affirmative action' bad words. By default, we let them destroy it. We can't just let that go. The majority has to, at some point, come to grips with the fundamental issue of unfairness in society. We have to go back to holding their feet to the fire on all these issues. We will never be a great world, never mind nation, until we address this issue of racism."

During his speech on justice in America later that night, Cochran elaborated on these themes. He talked about the prevalence of racial profiling by police, and the unwritten criminal offence known as DWB, or "driving while black." He also mentioned a recent incident in which white firefighters marred a parade with a float that parodied the dragging death of a black man. He exhorted the audience to speak out, to become "advocates for justice."

The Johnnie Cochran who came to Halifax was not the man who was the subject of a hatchet job disguised as a profile in a recent edition of *The Coast*. Robert MacGregor's article depicted Cochran as a race-baiting limousine chaser; a man who no longer cares about causes or cases that don't bolster his bank balance.

103

The man MacGregor described would not have spent 25 years trying to free an ex-Black Panther named Geronimo Pratt from a life sentence imposed for murders he did not commit.

And he would not have foregone his lucrative speaking fee to help a community of which he had never heard before the director of the IBM program sent him a letter last year.

MacGregor accused Cochran of playing the "race card." But we must never forget who it was that stacked the deck in the first place.

Taking it to the streets

A decade of protest

Unlike blacks in the U.S., African-Nova Scotians do not often carry out mass demonstrations as protests or to publicize matters that need immediate attention. The relatively small number of blacks here — about two per cent of the province's population, compared with 12 per cent in the U.S. — precludes big marches such as the ones in the American South during the 1960s.

But sometimes issues, large or small, do arise that galvanize not only blacks, but whites as well. That's when African-Nova Scotians raise their voices in dissent, as they did in the fall of 1990, when the Zellers store advertised the wrong kind of dolls.

Hundreds of marchers participate in anti-racism demonstration in August, 1991. *(Stu Ducklow/The Daily News)*

Choosing your 'toys' carefully
October 15, 1990

Old racial stereotypes don't fade away. They just keep resurfacing under different guises.

The latest guise may be found in a flyer distributed by Zellers last week. On the last page of that flyer there's an ad for Club Z, where supposedly "the best things in life are free."

If you have a Club Z card, you know the routine. Every time you make a purchase at Zellers, you get Club Z points. Once you accumulate enough of these points, you can redeem them for anything from an ashtray to a color TV.

According to last week's flyer, 40,000 points will get you a set of four "lovely hand-made porcelain dolls" that are "beautifully crafted." These items are available not only at Club Z, but also at the Zellers store in the Dartmouth Shopping Centre.

In reality, the dolls are crude caricatures of blacks, with big bug eyes and watermelon-eating grins. They are dressed in clothes that look like a cross between a pair of pyjamas and a clown outfit. They represent a stereotype that should have passed into history with Amos 'n' Andy.

Not only do these "lovely" dolls come with their own "carry pouches" — they even have names. Regular readers of this paper are now aware of what those names are: "Eeny, Meeny, Miney, and Moe."

Eeny, meeny, miney, moe. Nonsense syllables that are part of an old children's rhyme. In its entirety, the rhyme goes like this:

"Eeny, meeny, miney, moe,
Catch a nigger by the toe,
If he hollers let him go,
Eeny, meeny, miney, moe."

Of course, we didn't all learn that little ditty the same way. When I was a child, we substituted the word "tiger" for "nigger." I spent half my childhood wondering why anybody would be crazy enough to catch a tiger by the toe. Then I heard some white kids chanting it in its original form, and I got the picture.

That picture came back full-force when this matter was brought to my attention.

What's really interesting about the Club Z ad is that just below the four black dolls, you'll find three white ones. The Jesters, they're called. Three cherubic-faced little white dolls dressed in medieval court jester's outfits. The going rate for The Jesters is 50,000 Club Z points. Apparently, at Club Z three white dolls are worth more than four black ones.

What a subtle message . . .

Some may wonder why so much fuss is being made over a matter that might seem trivial on its surface. That was the reaction of local Zellers management when they were contacted by people from the black community. Complaints by Percy Paris and Jessica Bowden were met by a stone wall of indifference. Zellers officials did not see anything offensive about the dolls or their names. Requests for a printed apology and a removal of the dolls from Club Z's stock were summarily rejected. So was a request to take them off the shelves of the store in the Dartmouth Shopping Centre.

As a result of those rejections, a complaint has been filed at the Nova Scotia Human Rights Commission. And the Dartmouth store was picketed last Friday.

The dolls, of course, are not the only issue. They are symptomatic of a much larger problem.

Systemic racism is a term that refers to stereotyped attitudes that are so deeply ingrained in our culture that we often fail to recognize them for what they are. The case of "Eeny, Meeny, Miney, and Moe" is a textbook example of the way systemic racism works — beneath the surface, like a deadly virus that causes temporary blindness in racial matters.

That's why this matter is trivial only to those who lack even the slightest degree of empathy for minority concerns.

Why didn't anyone at Zellers or Club Z see anything wrong with the dolls or their names? Why does Zellers management resist efforts to make them understand exactly how offensive those four little dolls are? What rhymes did the people who sell those dolls sing during their childhood? Did they dream of catching tigers by the toe?

The flyers in question were delivered throughout metro and the Annapolis Valley. Reactions to the ad for the dolls has ranged from upset to outrage. But the most telling comment I've heard so far came from a woman who is a long-time Zellers customer: "I owe Zellers some money. But you know what? They can collect it from Eeny, Meeny, Miney, and Moe!"

Blacks, Zellers both winners
January 21, 1991

After nearly three months of negotiations, Zellers and the black community have resolved their dispute over the sale of racially-stereotyped dolls.

In a press release issued last week, the department store announced that it would sponsor events during this February's Black History Month. As well, Zellers will provide prizes for contests relating to black history. The store also apologized for having sold the set of Taiwan-made dolls, which were advertised under the derogatory names "Eeny, Meeny, Miney, and Moe," and admitted that its initial response to black community concerns was "insensitive."

The announcement came after a meeting that involved Zellers representatives, the Nova Scotia Human Rights Commission, and Percy Paris, the Dalhousie University professor who initiated the complaint. All three parties are happy with the result.

In retrospect, the incident progressed in three stages: resistance, retrenchment, and resolution. The first two stages unfolded within a week's time. The third took longer.

Resistance was Zellers' initial response when Paris and others first aired the black community's concern over the dolls. "We don't see any problem," store officials said. "The dolls are staying on the shelves." One spokesman went so far as to refer to the dolls as "cute."

That response was met by demonstrations, boycott threats, national media coverage, and a formal letter of complaint from the Canadian Ethnocultural Council. Protests occurred in both Dartmouth and Toronto.

Within a day of its original hard-line stance, Zellers beat a hasty retreat. The dolls were removed from store shelves, and a terse one-line statement was released apologizing for any offense that might have been taken.

However, that response wasn't really a resolution of the issue. In fact, it aggravated the situation because the store still refused to acknowledge the insulting nature of the dolls and their name (taken from a racist children's rhyme), or to take steps to prevent similar incidents from occurring in the future.

Intentional or not, Zellers' handling of the incident looked more like a public relations ploy than a sincere effort to redress a wrong.

Thus, retrenchment. Paris and other concerned members of the minority and majority communities settled in for what promised to be a protracted standoff with Zellers at the Human Rights Commission.

Instead, the conflict has ended amicably. Why? At some time during the past two months, an attitudinal sea change must have transpired in Zellers upper echelons. A sincere attempt to understand the minority's point of view led to the breakthrough that occurred last week.

Had Zellers done nothing more than sponsor black history events and donate prizes, charges of attempting to "buy off" the community might have been raised. However, the store has done much more than that.

Zellers regional vice-president Michael Monaghan announced a "strengthening" of his company's committment to affirmative action. There is also a good chance an affirmative action or employment equity officer will be hired. Employment equity was one of the key proposals Paris had brought into the negotiations.

And, in a fitting turn of the circle, Zellers will be stocking a selection of realistic black dolls, including black versions of the popular "Barbie" and "Newborn" models. For years, those dolls were relatively difficult to find. Zellers is doing a great service by making them available.

The positive outcome of this incident is not just a victory for Percy Paris, though he deserves a great deal of credit for his perseverance. And it's not just a victory for the black and other minority communities of Canada. It's also a victory for Zellers.

During the summer of 1991, the eviction of a black patron from a downtown Halifax bar triggered some of the worst racially motivated street violence the city had yet seen — followed by the largest peaceful demonstration in the history of Halifax. The short, hot summer of '91 focused attention on bar discrimination, tensions between blacks and police, and efforts of blacks and whites to defuse a racial powderkeg.

Racial barometer at a peak
July 22, 1991

What really happened on the streets of Halifax last Wednesday, Thursday, Friday, and Saturday nights?

The truth will have to be pieced together over a period of time. Witnesses see what they want to see, hear what they want to hear, remember what they want to remember. News reports have been contradictory and misleading, with details changing by the hour.

At this point, we do know there's been violent behavior in different parts of the city; that the violence has been for the most part racially-motivated; that the police have been called in; and that blacks and whites alike have been injured, hospitalized, and arrested.

Events began in a downtown Halifax bar, part of the drinker's paradise that rises like a rum cake between Barrington and Brunswick Streets. Hindsight has prompted some commentators to call this district a "flashpoint" because of long-standing complaints about discrimination against black patrons.

Several months ago, a downtown demonstration by the Cultural Awareness Youth Group resulted in a series of negotiations between bar owners and blacks, as well as a threat from the province to revoke the liquor licence of any establishment that practiced racial discrimination. After years of much talk and little action, genuine progress appeared to be underway.

But meetings and negotiations are one thing. The volatile combination of youth, booze, belligerence, race, and sex that permeates the downtown drinking scene is something else again.

Even that, however, doesn't adequately account for worst outbreak of racial violence since the fights at Cole Harbour District High School in 1989.

The violence on Wednesday and Thursday nights was an eruption of the tension that has existed ever since blacks and whites began living in North America.

Reports to date agree that Wednesday's incident occurred when a group of whites attacked a pair of blacks in Rosa's Cantina, one of the few overtly "integrated" downtown bars. The reason for the attack remains unknown. It was, however, the spark that set off the next night's explosive events.

What brought the crowd of blacks (with a few white buddies who went along for the ride) downtown that Thursday? Was it the fight itself? Was it the bar's alleged banning of the blacks involved in the altercation, but not the whites? Was it an accumulation of frustration, anger, bitterness, and resentment at being trapped within one's own skin; a burden that could be borne no longer?

It was all that, and more — motivations that were understandable, leading to behavior that was inexcusable.

The police had to act. No one could expect them to sit tight in the station when more than 100 people were rampaging in the streets. In situations like this, the police often find themselves in a no-win position. If they do too little, they are criticized for failing to do their job. If they do too much, they get accused of brutality.

Still, if witnesses' claims that the police waded into the rioters after community leaders had already calmed matters down are true, the police have some explaining to do. That kind of conduct undermines the credibility of both the police and the leaders who were only trying to prevent a bad situation from becoming worse. Unfortunately, the situation became worse just as the crowd was about to disperse.

What, then, can be learned from the past three nights of fury?

The leaders, the church groups, the political advocacy organizations, the self-help groups, even the angry, window-smashing youths — everyone is fighting for the same cause. It is a cause for which we have struggled for centuries. As the old spiritual eloquently puts it, we seek the right to sing our song in a strange land.

Still, there are correct and incorrect ways to go about singing that song.

The bottom line is, you don't attack innocent people who aren't bothering you. You don't break up other people's property. You don't trash your own neighborhood.

Once those things start to happen, our song is sung off-key and our cause goes flying out the window along with the broken glass. Then society's spotlight shines no longer on the injustices others have perpetrated on us, but on the injustices we perpetrate on others.

And that doesn't help anybody.

In the days that followed the disturbance, tensions remained high, as did the potential for further violence. Several black community leaders decided explosive tempers could be defused, and the issues that underlay the tensions emphasized, through a peaceful march against racism. Some people felt the march would only invite more trouble. However, march organizers prevailed, and on a hot day in August, a step into history was taken.

The big march:
Every step made history
August 4, 1991

August 1, 1991 ....

It's about ten after five in the afternoon, and here we are at the George Dixon Community Centre on Gottingen Street. Said in the paper we supposed to gather here at 5:30. Figured we'd be the first ones here, but there's plenty of others. Black folks, white folks, old, young, and in-between. More coming all the time in ones and twos and small groups.

Some call this a peace march. Others call it an anti-racism rally. Others call it premature. Whatever else you want to call it, you'll have to call it big before it's over. Here it is, only a little past 5:30, and the grounds outside the Dixon Centre are filling up faster than a #1 Spring Garden bus at rush hour.

Plenty of blacks are out here. And a lot more whites.

Don't see anybody in charge here yet, but the people are getting along just fine. Listen to that roar up on Gottingen. Whole line of police motorcycles coming to escort us down the street. Here come the arm-banded marshals from the Cultural Awareness Youth Group. There's Darryl Gray, talking with a bullhorn, getting us started.

113

They said the march was going to begin at 6:00. It's 6:00 now, and we're moving. Young folks are out front, carrying banners that stretch halfway across the street. Drums are rolling, and a trumpet's playing "When The Saints Go Marching In."

We're going past the senior citizens' homes. They're out on the front steps, waving and smiling. One man gives us the "V" for victory sign. Nobody's given us just half of it yet.

The chants are starting:

> *What do you want?*
> *Justice!*
> *When do you want it?*
> *Now!*
> *What do you want?*
> *Equality!*
> *When do you want it?*
> *Now!*

Here we go past Uniacke Square. People are lined up on the sidewalks, cheering us on. Some of them are coming across the street and joining us. The ones who don't join the march are looking a little shocked at the number of people they're seeing. Nobody expected this kind of turnout.

We're past Cogswell now, going up the little hill in front of the police station. Look back down there! You can't see the end of the crowd! Even the oldest people in the march can't remember seeing anything like this before.

That little route map that got published in the paper says we're supposed to be going to Argyle past the Grand Parade, then up Sackville to South Park. Guess they don't want us to be walking past those bars where all the trouble started.

Whoa! Look at the front of the line! They're changing direction. We're not going up Sackville after all. We're staying right on Argyle.

> *Hey hey! Ho ho!*
> *Racism has got to go!*
> *Hey hey! Ho ho!*
> *Racism has got to go!*

If there's going to be trouble on this march, it'll most likely happen here. It's early, though. Too early in the evening for the drinking crowd. It's the dining crowd that's peering at us from the terraces and windows.

On the sidewalks, there's young men and women wearing bar staff uniforms. Some of them look at us with deadpan stares, but others are smiling, clapping, and cheering us on. There's not a black face among them.

We go down Argyle, up Blowers, and double back along Grafton, passing most of Halifax's major watering holes and making our point with our presence. By the time the head of the line begins to climb Sackville, the end is still coming down Duke. We must have doubled our numbers since we started. Already there's estimates of 1,000, 1,500, even 2,000.

And there's been no trouble so far. No taunts, no gestures, no blaring horns from the disrupted traffic we pass. It's as though the march has a power of its own — the power to open eyes and unplug ears.

Now we're back on our original route. First Sackville, then South Park. The south end of the city, where blacks are seldom seen and never heard. Until now.

> *Halifax, Halifax have you heard?*
> *This is not Johannesburg!*
> *Halifax, Halifax have you heard?*
> *This is not Johannesburg!*

Feet are getting sore. Throats are getting dry. Voices are getting hoarse. But tempers are not getting short, and resolve is not weakening. With each step, the significance of the march sinks in. Each step is a step that makes history.

There aren't as many onlookers on South Park as there were on Gottingen. But they're just as friendly. We pass an elderly white lady who leans on a cane. She has a big grin on her face, and her hand is waving back and forth, back and forth. The twinkle in her eyes says, "If I could throw down this cane, I'd be out there with you."

Finally we file into Huskies Stadium at St. Mary's University. Once we are seated, we will listen to speakers from a broad spectrum of political and social consciousness. And when the speeches are over, we will go home, reflect on what we have heard and done, and, perhaps, keep on marching in our minds.

Two wrongs make two wrongs
December 21, 1991

Topic for the day: the recent report issued by a police/civilian incident review committee on the conduct of the police during last summer's racial violence in downtown Halifax.

Thought for the day: two wrongs make — two wrongs.

Because of outrage from the black community concerning alleged racial slurs and brutality during police handling of the disturbances, Chief Vince MacDonald ordered an investigation of the incident. Three members of the black community — Mayann Francis and Reverends Donald Skeir and Calvin Symonds — formed the civilian component of the review team.

The committee's report has caused controversy because it's really two documents: one representing the police viewpoint, the other that of the civilian members. In terms of mutual agreement, the two sides were about as far apart as the Israelis and Palestinians. The entire exercise was like a dialogue between people who aren't speaking the same language.

Example:

Police: "Police response was controlled and well-managed."

Blacks: "We're not at all convinced that the various investigations were appropriately conducted."

At this point, it's important to make one thing clear. The violence against people and property in downtown Halifax and on Gottingen Street was wrong. No responsible person would suggest that the police should have stayed in their station that night. It was their duty to quell the disturbance.

The main question raised in the aftermath was relatively straightforward: Did the police do their duty in a fair, unbiased manner? The incident review committee bore the responsibility of attempting to address that concern. Unfortunately, its report only raises more questions, such as, "Can the wide chasm between the way blacks and whites perceive each other ever be bridged?"

The answer is, "It can." But the construction of that bridge is going to take a great deal of hard work from both sides.

More dialogue:

Blacks: "Every time we point out incidents of racism on the part of the police, they say they're just 'doing their job'."

Police: "We're tired of being called 'racist' every time we try to do our job."

This cycle of accusation and denial occurs in all aspects of society; it isn't restricted to the police. Most whites resent being accused of racism. Outside of those who burn crosses and wear swastikas, most people, regardless of their color, accept the premise that racism is at best immoral and at worst evil. Naturally, one's first impulse when confronted with an accusation of racism is to deny it, then question the motivations of the accuser.

From the black perspective, it is sometimes difficult to distinguish which is worse — acts of racism themselves, or the disavowals that invariably follow such acts. True, there are times when blacks perceive racism that isn't really there. But racism is reality in so many cases that it has to be taken into consideration in every aspect of a black or other minority individual's life. And to be confronted with repeated refusals to even consider the possibility of discrimination or out-and-out racism in cases like the July disturbance can be extremely frustrating.

Still, the fact that an investigative committee was formed at all is a step in the right direction. And, to his credit, Chief MacDonald has indicated that he is willing to consider re-opening investigations into allegations of racial slurs and discrimination. Whatever the final outcome, those allegations must be taken seriously. The three black members of the committee are reliable, trustworthy individuals; they are not the type to issue irresponsible accusations just to get their names in the paper.

Smashing windows and beating up innocent people is wrong.

Abusing the power and responsibility involved in enforcing the law (*let's throw this nigger off the bridge*) is also wrong.

And two wrongs make — two wrongs.

When Jean Chrétien's federal Liberals took power in 1993, they found the nation's finances in dire straits. To eliminate the budget deficit, many social programs were axed. The process continued through the Liberals' first mandate, and in 1996, a Canada Employment Centre office in North End Halifax received notice that it was scheduled to be closed. However, the feds had not reckoned with the reaction of North End residents and their friends.

Centre was a hub of hope
April 4, 1996

Why are they downsizing the downsized? That question came to mind late last month, when the closing of the Canada Employment Centre on Gottingen Street was announced. Human Resources Development Canada said a smaller office to be located at the Community YMCA would replace it, but some services would be available only at the main employment centre located in the Halifax Shopping Centre.

In operation for two decades, the centre has been a hub of hope in an area that has undergone more than its share of setbacks during that time. Gottingen Street, the focal point of the North End, has lost a supermarket, department store and two cinemas over the past few years. The community has suffered a high jobless rate. Estimates of the unemployment percentage among blacks who live in the North End range as high as 70 per cent.

The North End is not an all-black area, but it does have a larger concentration of blacks than other areas of the city. For residents of all backgrounds, the CEC office has provided a lifeline that leads to a job.

With governments at all levels reducing their social-programs spending, unemployment insurance and welfare are being cut — and so was a service mandated to help people avoid UI and welfare. The downsized were being downsized, and concerned people from Dalhousie Legal Aid to the African Canadian Caucus to the Public Service Alliance of Canada asked a simple question: "Why?"

Answers ranged from bureaucratic insensitivity to systemic racism; neglect of the poor to deficit-fighting mania. Speculation over the reasons the government made its decision could go on forever, resolving nothing.

118

So those who were concerned asked a second, more complicated question: "What can we do about it?"

The Gottingen Street centre was scheduled to shut its doors at the end of last month. Officially, the centre is now closed.

But in reality, it is still occupied — not by its former staff, but by protesters who decided direct action was the answer to the second question.

A week after the closing was announced, more than a dozen people entered the CEC office and began a sit-in that continues today. Other protesters have held a series of marches outside the building. After the office shut down as scheduled and the staffers went on to other assignments, the protesters stayed put. They have remained despite a visit last Sunday by CEC officials and Halifax police officers.

These demonstrators are not simply taking up space. They are asking the government to reopen the office on a temporary basis while a plan is devised to keep a full-service, full-time employment centre on Gottingen Street.

Earlier this week, the protesters offered their own employment counselling, although the hours involved were limited.

Negotiations continue. Human Resources officials say the Gottingen Street center will not be reopened. But they're going to have to find a new location for their substitute centre, since the YMCA announced it will not provide space for it.

And the protesters say they won't move until their demands are met.

The demonstration has been peaceful, co-operative, and constructive. It has pulled diverse elements of the community together in a way that has not been seen since the massive march against racism that was held here during the summer of 1991. Although media images have tended to focus on the black participants in the protest, blacks and whites alike have been involved in both the sit-in and the marches.

The protesters are not asking for a handout for the North End. They are asking the federal government not to withdraw the helping hand the CEC has extended to the community for the past 20 years.

Because of political and social circumstances decades in the making, blacks and everyone else in the North End have endured employment difficulties during good and bad economic times. These are bad times, and those at the bottom of the economic ladder all too often see a broken rung above them and oblivion below. A fully-staffed employment office is often the first rung on the ladder for North End residents. The government should not break it or take it away.

The question remains: Why downsize the downsized?

North End rallies around CEC protest
April 21, 1996

To paraphrase the great African-American poet Langston Hughes, "Whatever happens to a dream denied?" One answer to that question can be found at the office of the Canada Employment Centre on Gottingen Street.

What began as a spontaneous sit-in to protest the federal government's plan to close the centre last month is quickly growing into a full-fledged social-protest movement.

Chances are, not even the organizers anticipated that their cause would gain the strong support it has received so far. And it's very likely that Human Resources Canada (HRC), the government agency responsible for the employment centres, believed that after the demonstrators let off steam and made their point, they'd go home and the universe would unfold as it should.

Well, something is unfolding. But it isn't quite what the deficit-cutters in Ottawa may have had in mind.

The closing seemed routine at first, as have so many other cutbacks. The full-service Gottingen Street office would be shut down. A smaller, partial-service facility would be temporarily housed in the Community YMCA on Gottingen Street. Otherwise, people living in North End Halifax would have to travel to the main CEC office at the Halifax Shopping Centre to receive services that were previously only a few blocks' walk away.

But the Gottingen Street centre wasn't just another government office filled with people pushing paper. The North End has long been plagued by a high unemployment rate, especially among its black residents. For many, the centre provided the first step up from a rut of poverty and disillusion. To have that step taken away in the name of deficit reduction inflicted a heavy blow on the community.

Trimming the fat from the government to save taxpayers' money is a laudable goal. But the Gottingen Street CEC office isn't fat. It's part of the North End's heart and soul.

The North End has been knocked down before. The closings of the neighborhood supermarket and department store drew blood, as did the vandalism that occurred during a racial disturbance — sometimes called a "riot" — in the summer of 1991.

But every time the people of the area are knocked down, they get back up again. Sometimes they just dust themselves off and keep on going. At other times, they battle back.

A few weeks after the 1991 "riot," Gottingen Street was filled with hundreds of people peacefully marching against racism. The march remains one of the largest demonstrations of its kind Halifax has ever seen.

Since the CEC office closed, there have been several protest rallies in front of its doors, as well as the sit-in. The occupation of the centre continues despite a visit from police in its earliest days.

The rallies haven't attracted the numbers that stretched as far as the eye could see in 1991. But the support the centre's cause has attracted in and out of the North End has been just as impressive. The support has come in a number of ways:

The landlord of the office offered to cut its rent and provide renovations. Also, the landlord has not objected to the continued presence of the occupiers.

Soon after the protest began, the YMCA announced it would not house the smaller CEC after all.

The Halifax Regional Municipality tabled a resolution asking Human Resources Minister Doug Young to send his staff "back to the bargaining table with the protesters" and "reopen the centre until a study can determine whether or not it is needed in the community."

Halifax church leaders sent a letter of protest to Young asking him to "find a solution that meets the community's needs and the government's objectives."

Artworks, an association of local artists, held a parade and performance in support of the protest yesterday.

Provincial Environment Minister Wayne Adams, who grew up in the North End, has written to Young asking him to meet with the protesters to "determine a long-term solution to an HRDC service facility on Gottingen Street."

The protesters, who have occupied the centre for 26 days, have held off-and-on talks with HRC officials. A recent letter from Young has prompted a resumption of negotiations.

Advice to Young and Human Resources Canada: Reopen the centre. Don't deny a beleaguered community's dream of self-improvement.

You will not be backing down. You will not be giving in. You will not be setting a dangerous precedent.

You will only be doing what a government is supposed to do — helping people to help themselves.

Victory on Gottingen Street
August 4, 1996

The outcome of a 122-day sit-in at the Canada Employment Centre on Gottingen Street should not be viewed in terms of winners and losers, even though on the surface it would appear that the protesters won and the federal government lost.

Late last month Human Resources Development Canada, which had closed the centre at the end of March, announced that it would re-open as a full-service employment office. However, that is only a temporary measure. The deal, mediated by the North End Council of Churches, calls for an assessment to be done of the community's employment-services needs, to be followed by recommendations for a permanent policy.

This result isn't about winning or losing. It's about doing the right thing.

Although the centre was back in business as of last Monday, "re-open" may not be the most appropriate word to use here. After all, despite the earlier shutdown order, the office was never really closed.

In March, HRDC announced the termination of the two-decade-old institution as a cost-cutting measure. A smaller CEC office was to be housed at the Community YMCA on Maitland Street. For full job-seeking services, however, people in the North End of Halifax would have to travel to a centre located at the Halifax Shopping Centre — not exactly walking distance.

122

The North End community reacted swiftly and vehemently. Criticism of HRDC's move was threefold:

With unemployment in the area running at a high level, what sense did it make to cut back on a job-finding service?

The area has a large black population, upon whom the consequences of the centre's closing would have a disproportionate impact.

The closing was the latest in a long series of departures by offices and businesses from once-thriving Gottingen Street.

Those and many other words were spoken in the weeks before the centre was slated to close. But words would not be enough to stop what amounted to a wrong-headed bureaucratic judgment.

On March 29, the centre's doors were to be closed. On March 27, 15 protesters — people from the North End community and their sympathizers — entered the office and began an occupation that lasted nearly four months.

The purpose of the sit-in was to reverse the decision HRDC had made. At a time when the national unemployment rate remained close to the 10-per-cent level, and the North End rate several times higher than that, the area needed the centre more than ever.

Perhaps local HRDC officials believed the protest would peter out once the people occupying the office had vented their anger and publicized their point. That didn't happen.

As time passed, more people joined the cause and their determination grew stronger. Indeed, both sides dug in their heels for a long grapple. The protesters may not have sung the civil rights anthem "Ain't Gonna Let Nobody Turn Me 'Round," but they remained true to its spirit.

The threat of eviction by police didn't turn them around. The government's initial intransigence didn't turn them around. The discomforts and inconveniences involved in a 24-hour-a-day occupation didn't turn them around.

As well, the occupiers never changed their position. Their goal was to keep the office open as a full-service employment centre until an acceptable alternative could be found through a decision-making process that involved input from the community.

That goal remained paramount even as the government counter-attacked. HRDC's arguments were that all government departments were under pressure to pare their costs as part of an effort to eliminate the federal deficit; that the Gottingen Street CEC was not the only such office to close in Canada; that other areas in need of employment centres did not have them; that the Gottingen Street centre had been under-used.

The protesters hung tough against all those contentions. They brought attention to their cause through street rallies and news conferences. And the tide of public opinion moved toward them and against the federal government, particularly Human Resources Development Minister Doug Young and Halifax-riding MP Mary Clancy. Clancy was singled out for "neglecting" the area and taking a hard line against the protesters.

Negotiations between the protesters and the government started, stopped and started again. Government representatives said they couldn't continue negotiations while the protesters were occupying the office; the protesters said they wouldn't leave until an acceptable deal was made.

The standoff finally ended with the agreement brokered by the church group. The story isn't over yet; the results of the assessment process must satisfy both sides. But so far, the protest appears to have fulfilled its purpose.

The CEC centre continues to serve Halifax's North End community.

School days:
The sequel

Violence returns with a vengeance

During the first half of the 1990s, racial tensions at Cole Harbour High School remained out of the headlines. In late 1996, however, violence between white and black students erupted once again, and the spotlight of media publicity again cast its glare on the troubled school, and spread to another. Of course, the students who had participated in the 1989 brawls were long gone, but a new generation had inherited their anger.

Students gather in front of Cole Harbour High School after October, 1997 mêlée. *(Paul Darrow/The Daily News)*

School fight *déjà vu* in black and white
November 3, 1996

Once again, a racial brawl at Cole Harbour High School makes head-lines and spurs debate. The moment the news got out last month that whites and blacks were fighting at the large suburban school, memories flashed back to the winter of 1989, when a televised fray created repercussions that reverberate to this day.

Once again, whites from Eastern Passage traded blows with blacks from North Preston.

Once again, non-students from both communities were involved.

Once again, the majority of students, black and white alike, wondered if violence would await them when they returned to class.

However, after the initial tingle of *déjà vu* fades, it's clear that Cole Harbour II is not a sequel to Cole Harbour I. Beneath the surface similarities, there are significant differences.

The 1989 incident was racial from start to finish — a snowball fight between black and white students escalated into two days of racially motivated violence.

Last month's clash began with a dispute over drugs. The principals were split along racial lines, but drug money, not race, was the motivating factor. Only when the conflict was carried into the school did some students jump to racial conclusions, then jump into the fight.

Another parallel: in both brawls, whites and blacks faced charges. Ten blacks and eight whites were charged with unlawful assembly and creating a disturbance in the 1989 incident. Last month, police laid charges of assault and causing a disturbance against three whites and two blacks.

The disposition of the 1989 charges led to lingering resentments among blacks. Of the 10 whites charged, none was convicted. Three blacks were convicted. One was invalidated because the Crown did not properly lay the charge. The others took their case to the Nova Scotia Court of Appeal, which in 1993 ruled against them.

The two men argued that the RCMP investigation of the brawls was incomplete because most of its interviews were with white witnesses, thus creating a racially biased body of evidence. The appeal judges disagreed. The outcome left the impression that whites are more likely to go free and blacks are likely to do time for similar crimes.

Mindful of that perception, RCMP officers have done a more complete investigation of the October incident, interviewing black and white witnesses. That means there will be less reason to believe that racial bias played a role in the legal process, regardless of the outcome.

Another difference is the community response to the violence. In 1989, attempts at conciliation between black and white parents were preceded by a period of accusation and name-calling.

This time, conciliation began immediately, with prayer meetings at the school as well as churches in Eastern Passage and North Preston. Resentment on both sides is either non-existent or seething beneath a calm surface.

So far, Cole Harbour II is being dealt with better than Cole Harbour I by the school, the police, and the communities.

Hopefully, the outcome of Cole Harbour II will ensure there won't be a Cole Harbour III sometime in the future.

Cole Harbour III occurred less than two months later.

Putting wings on wishes won't solve Metro's race problems
December 22, 1996

If race had not been the main element in relations between blacks and whites in North America for the past three centuries, it would never have mattered in the latest violence at Cole Harbour High School.

If skin color meant no more than hair color, the fight at the school's Christmas dance and the subsequent police response would not have joined a long line of racial incidents in Nova Scotia.

And if wishes were wings . . . well, you know the rest.

History has left a legacy of race and racism, which are two different things. Race is a fact; racism an attitude. The collision of facts and attitudes can lead to misunderstanding — and violence.

The role of race breaks down to three levels: primary, secondary, and peripheral.

At the primary level, race is the main motivating factor.

At the secondary level, race plays a role, even if it isn't the original cause.

At the peripheral level, race is a minor concern.

These levels apply equally to blacks and whites.

The racial factor in the violence at the school dance began at the peripheral level. Two girls — one white, one black — got into a shoving match. According to information available so far, race was not the reason the scuffle started. If the altercation had broken up quickly, with no one else involved, it would not have escalated into a full-fledged brawl.

And if wishes were wings ....

Others did intervene, and were attacked. At least one intervenor was white; the attackers were black. Race became a factor as participation in the melee broadened. At that point, the incident still might have been defused. Faculty supervising the dance say they had the fighting under control. But some students called the police and, as one witness put it, "all hell broke loose."

The job of the police is to calm troubled waters. But in this case, the actions of RCMP and other units brought troubled waters to a boil. The bare bones of what happened after the police cars arrived are as follows: The first officers to answer the call were swarmed. Two were injured. One said he felt someone reaching for his gun. Backup was called. The police used pepper spray and batons to subdue the crowd. Two youths were taken to hospital. Five blacks were arrested. Whites were allowed to stay inside the school; blacks were herded outside.

Beyond the bare bones, comments from witnesses follow a "we-said, they-said" pattern.

The police say they behaved appropriately in stopping the fight and defending themselves against their attackers, and race had nothing to do with their actions.

School authorities say police "over-reacted."

Black students and parents say the police singled out blacks in a fracas that involved both races. One parent, Rev. Darryl Gray, said police grabbed and threatened him when he asked questions about the arrests.

Gray has also been a whipping-boy for *Daily News* letter-writers who support the police. It's as though they think if only Gray would shut up, the race issue would fly away.

Yet Gray's admonishments were not one-sided. Last week, he told *The Herald* what he said to young black people about dealing with the police: "Let them do their job. Don't think every police officer you come into contact with is a racist or will do something bad to you. Give them a chance."

Are those the words of a person out to incite blacks against the police? Gray should be commended for having the courage to speak despite attempts to make him a scapegoat.

Columnist Arnie Patterson has written that in violent incidents between blacks and police, "blacks themselves" should bear some of the responsibility. Maybe he doesn't understand that blacks are among the most self-critical people the world has known. But what do we do after we've beaten ourselves up?

Obviously, the blacks who attacked the police officers singled themselves out for retaliation. It would be ludicrous to argue that the police should not have arrested them.

On the other hand, targeting blacks for arrest and separating the crowd by race created the appearance of a primary racial incident. Now, some blacks are calling for the closing of the RCMP's community-policing office in the Preston area. That would be a mistake. The office has only been open since May; it deserves more time before its future is decided.

Race is a reality. Relations between blacks in North Preston and the police remain volatile. Tension between white and black students at Cole Harbour High continues.

Those problems will not be solved by putting wings on wishes. Denial won't make race fly away. Neither will the inflammatory comments made last week by an RCMP spokesman and a metro councillor.

At a news conference, RCMP Inspector Wayne Pilgrim said officers have received threats from North Preston residents and some are afraid to go into the community because they consider it too dangerous.

"Those comments really disturb me," North Preston resident Morton Simmonds said last week. "The RCMP have no reason to be afraid to come here. Nobody's going to hurt them. I'll stand right beside them if they're doing the right thing."

Simmonds added: "But if they're doing the wrong thing, I'll go straight to the RCMP office and let them know."

RCMP officers have been sent on missions to Haiti and Bosnia, two of the world's worst trouble spots. Is North Preston more dangerous than Haiti or Bosnia?

The police may want to defend themselves against accusations they consider unfair. But doing it this way is like putting out fires with gasoline.

Then Cole Harbour North Councillor Ron Cooper suggested Cole Harbour High should be broken up because it "put together groups that just can't get along."

Is Cooper suggesting a return to segregated schools? What's next? "White" and "Colored" signs on washroom doors?

All sides in this impasse — black students, white students, black parents, white parents, and the police — need to take a hard look at themselves, then begin the demanding work necessary to heal the wounds events of the past year have ripped open.

Auburn Drive High School was built in the Cole Harbour area to relieve over-crowding. For the first few years of its existence, the new school remained free from the racial notoriety of its neighbor. In March of 1997, however, Auburn Drive High made headlines of its own.

Ignore the mixed messages
March 16, 1997

Throughout the latter part of 1996 and the beginning of this year, violent racial incidents at Cole Harbour District High School made headlines. Now, the spotlight has shifted to another school in the same area — Auburn Drive High.

Students at Auburn Drive received an extended March Break after racial unrest on March 5 that included fights, and shouting and shoving matches. Nine police cars responded to the incident, and charges are being considered against a 17-year-old black male student and a 19-year-old white male non-student. Last Friday, nine students were suspended for their involvement in the incident.

After March Break ends tomorrow, teachers and administrators at the school will face the unenviable task of easing racial tensions that have built up over a relatively short time. Some students and parents say media reports on black student dissatisfaction sparked the violence. But that's a superficial view; the roots of the unrest lie well beneath the surface.

Auburn Drive High School was conceived in 1993 to alleviate over-crowding at Cole Harbour District High School. At that time, some parents in the Preston-Cherry Brook black communities expressed fears that the new school would become a haven for whites seeking to distance themselves from black students. The decision to create the new school came only a few years after the notorious 1989 racial brawls at Cole Harbour High; within that context, the black parents' concerns were understandable.

In April 1993, a review committee of what was then the Halifax County-Bedford School Board recommended boundaries that would provide "a good cultural, social and economic mix of the community" in the student bodies of both high schools. Blacks now account for approximately 10 per cent of Auburn Drive's population.

Is there safety in those numbers? Perhaps. But some black students have said they are encountering old problems at the new school.

Gyasi Symonds, a Grade 12 student at the school, told a panel discussion about an essay he wrote for African Heritage Month. The topic he chose was the lack of black studies in the curriculum. Symonds was not allowed to read his essay at the opening of the school's African Heritage Month celebration.

In defence of that decision, Auburn Drive's principal, Don Buck, told *The Herald*: "Some of the aspects were more of a negative tone in terms of black-white relationships, and we were trying to focus on celebration."

African Heritage Month is indeed a time of celebration. It's a celebration of black people's triumph over adversity. During African Heritage Month, the triumph should be emphasized. But the adversity should not be ignored.

Symonds's essay wasn't read at the opening ceremonies because the principal didn't want to upset anyone. Yet racial tensions at the school didn't go away.

On March 3, *The Chronicle-Herald* ran a story about a group of black parents who joined forces to fight what they believe to be "subtle racism" that "is not creating a positive learning environment for our children." One anonymous black parent expressed her concerns in blunt terms: "It seems to me in that school they don't want black children. They want to repress them so they can get in trouble so they can get suspended or get so discouraged that they leave."

The day after *The Herald* story appeared, anger filled the halls of Auburn Drive High. Some black students — and parents — felt the article had accurately represented their grievances. Some whites thought the report was unfair to them. That race-based difference in perception echoes black and white reactions to coverage of violence at Cole Harbour High.

School board member Stephen Boyce added fuel to the fire when he made the following comment to *The Daily News* in reference to black parents' concerns: "Maybe it's time for people to look in the mirror and stop crying racism to justify the actions of their children every time they break the rules."

What a mixed message that is. Normally, parents are encouraged to become actively involved in their children's education. Such involvement benefits teachers and students alike. But when black parents actively protest racism in the education system, they are told to "look in the mirror" and "stop crying 'racism'." The parents of black students at Auburn Drive High — and every other school in Nova Scotia — should ignore mixed messages and continue to fight racism wherever they see it. They should do everything they can to ensure their children are gaining all the benefits school integration was intended to bestow.

Schools are not isolated environments. They reflect the reality of the rest of the world. If racism exists outside the schools, it will exist inside as well.

Anyone who denies that reality is looking into a mirror that has no glass.

Halls of hope and anger
April 13, 1997

Before the walkout last week of more than 30 black students at Auburn Drive High School, memories of earlier racially charged fights at that school and Cole Harbour High were melting like snow in the springtime. But for students, parents and teachers at those schools, cold reality persists.

The students who walked out last Thursday complained that Auburn High's principal, Don Buck, had not honored their request for a meeting to discuss the school's racial problems.

On Friday, Buck met with the students. However, that meeting would not have occurred if their parents had not persuaded them to return to the school.

Roy Clayton is chairman of the Parents Support Group for Auburn Drive School. The East Preston resident's daughter is an Auburn Drive student, and he has nieces and nephews there as well. All but one of the support group's members are black. The lone white member is the mother of a bi-racial child.

Clayton wants the public to understand why parents of black students find it necessary to form a separate group to speak out against the negative experiences some of their children are undergoing at the school. Several days before last week's walkout, he expressed his feelings, and those of the rest of the group, in this statement:

"We as the parents of Auburn Drive High School in Cole Harbour feel that the administration needs to be held accountable for the damage they have done to our children and students. They have abused them physically and mentally, and we give our children 100 per cent assurance that we would no longer tolerate that nonsense. We take the burdens off their shoulders and put them on ours. When they hurt, we hurt. When they cry, we cry. Enough is enough."

The group formed in late February, before last month's headline-grabbing fights and shouting matches between black and white students at Auburn Drive High.

"We saw our children having problems, and we decided to get together to try to do something," Clayton says. "The problems have been going on for a long time, and we were dealing with them one-on-one. Then we formed a group."

A story about that group appeared in *The Chronicle-Herald* and *Mail-Star* at the beginning of March. The story outlined black parents' concerns about "subtle racism" at Auburn Drive that "is not creating a positive learning environment for our children."

Race-related stories appear frequently in both *The Daily News* and *The Herald* newspapers, and their content has undoubtedly been discussed in heated terms on more than a few occasions. For some reason, though, the one about the black parents' support group became a lit match tossed on tinder.

The tinder was not the entire Auburn Drive student body; it was just those few sticks of wood — white and black — who were ready to ignite at the slightest provocation. Once the spark struck, the flames of anger spread, and in the aftermath nine students — seven of them black — received suspensions lasting up to five days.

Despite the presence of a race relations officer at the school, attempts at reconciliation have led to recrimination. The administration and some school board members have gone into a full-court defensive press. Their line is that black students do not have a race problem; they have a discipline problem, both in the school and at home. Black parents, they say, should stop "yelling racism" and make a greater effort to control their children's behavior. Of course, nothing is mentioned about any "discipline problems" the white students who participated in the shouting and the brawls may have had . . .

The situation is difficult. But the parents' support group is determined to help their children to obtain the education they will need in the knowledge-driven world of the future. And they want to remove any obstacles racism places in their children's path.

"Racism is an illness," Clayton says. "But illnesses can be cured."

How?

Clayton suggests direct involvement in the education system by black parents. "People from our group ought to be allowed to go into the classrooms to help with discipline and teach others about our community."

He does not believe a recent suggestion of bringing police into the schools will be helpful, because blacks would feel they were being targeted. Of more immediate concern to Clayton is the suspensions resulting from last month's violence. He thinks the suspensions were unfair. "We want them taken off the students' records."

These parents need to be heard. Their voices may be loud, but their frustration runs deep. Their concerns are the same as any other parents' concerns. But race is an extra burden, and they are doing the best they can to ensure that their children will not have to bear it.

The administration, school board and other authorities need to ask themselves whether their comments and actions are easing the burden — or adding to its weight.

Another view of the Auburn fight
August 17, 1997

The racial unrest at Auburn Drive High School is in the news again. No, there haven't been further outbreaks of violence at the school during its summer activities. However, a look at the cover of the July/August issue of *This Magazine* will bring back memories of the tension that gripped the school earlier this year.

The cover design shows faces of young blacks against a target-like background. The main headline: Fight at Auburn High, with the word "fight" printed in blood-red ink.

Further information under the headline says: A black-against-white brawl at a Nova Scotia high school paints a scary picture of racism in the classroom. The story was written by Ann Bains, a Toronto freelancer.

While metro media reports at the time of the fight focused on the behavior and opinions of parents, school administrators and the police who were called to break up the brawl, Bains puts the students — mostly black, but some whites as well — in the spotlight. She provides them the opportunity to express views that were overlooked when Auburn Drive High was in the headlines.

Generally, the students talk past each other on racial issues, as do far too many adults. Black students want whites to acknowledge racism; white students want blacks to get lost.

Bains places the problems Auburn's black students face within a historical context that is all too often forgotten. She recognizes that education "has been one of the most critical battlegrounds for black activists in Nova Scotia," dating back to the 1800s. And she lists the familiar, dismal statistics on the black Nova Scotian dropout and unemployment rates — a litany of woes similar to those found in most North American black communities.

The tone of Bains' article is more pessimistic than hopeful, mainly because she doesn't believe the school system is committed to the implementation of changes recommended by race-relations advisers.

Still, no one can simply walk away from the problem.

If you asked most African-Canadians or Americans to describe in one word what the best solution to the problems of their communities would be, the majority would say: education. Blacks see education as the key, the panacea, the Holy Grail. Huge amounts of money and energy have been spent in getting black children into — or keeping them out of — "good schools." The unspoken definition of "good" is "predominantly white," but there is no reason a predominantly black school cannot be "good."

Major battles are being fought over the desegregation and resegregation of the education system. The busing of minority students to "good" schools has caused riots in the streets. Proposals for Afrocentric schools have been scorned as "reverse racism." Questions are many; answers few.

In one telling moment, Bains says she is "pressed to find black faces" in the 1996-97 Auburn school yearbook. But, as she waits at the administration office for a student to arrive for an interview, she notices others "nervously waiting for the vice-principal to call them in to discuss discipline problems. All of them are black."

It would be difficult to find a better example of a cause-and-effect relationship. Send a student to the office enough times, and eventually he or she will walk out the door.

Discipline in the classroom, halls, and cafeteria is necessary. But, as in the case of the legal system, justice must not only be done, but seen to be done. Singling out one group as chronic malcontents for racial reasons is not discipline; it's discrimination.

Still, it would be as foolish to deny the educational progress blacks have made over the past 30 years as it would be to paper over the problems that still exist.

Some black students have taken advantage of the benefits "good schools" provide. They avoid the "discipline problem" pigeonhole, disprove the "inferior ability" stereotype, and receive recognition for their talent and hard work. They clear the hurdles racism places in their path, and after graduation they go on to lead productive lives, fulfilling the dreams of those who fought to make the opportunity possible. They are held up as examples of the success that awaits those who apply themselves. But in reality, they are survivors who have succeeded against the odds.

For far too many others, the benefits are an illusion and the odds insurmountable. They may apply themselves in the beginning, but they soon trip over the hurdles and fall into the pigeonholes. They only recognition they get is when they are summoned to the disciplinary office or suspended, expelled, or arrested. Unless they turn their lives around once their school days are over, as some manage to do, they become part of the sad statistics Bains mentions.

There are two ways a school — any school, not just Auburn Drive High — can be "good" for blacks. One is to preserve and enhance the opportunities it provides — an admittedly difficult task in an era of budget cuts, but necessary nonetheless. The other is to dismantle the hurdles, discard the pigeonholes and shelve the stereotypes. Those tasks are also difficult. But if they are not at least attempted, the consequences will be more tension, more violence, and more "scary" articles in *This* and other magazines.

The rest of the school year ended without further violence. In the fall of 1997, however, Cole Harbour High exploded yet again.

Answering the bell
October 12, 1997

The trouble at Cole Harbour District High School can no longer be viewed as a series of skirmishes between undisciplined students. Recent violent events there have revealed that matters are not, and have never been, that simple.

It's not just fisticuffs in the schoolyard. It's a clash of communities, cultures, and values. It's a collision of solitudes: each side convinced that its attitudes and behavior are wrapped in the raiment of righteousness; each equally certain that the people on the other side are so demonic they deserve either isolation or destruction — or both.

Israelis and Palestinians. Bosnian Serbs and Muslims. Irish Protestants and Catholics.

Eastern Passage and North Preston?

Can the feud between those communities, one white, the other black, in what used to be Halifax County, be compared with the most intransigent trouble spots in the world?

In terms of the level of violence, of course not. In terms of the intensity of the mutual dislike . . . maybe.

The animosity between these two solitudes did not begin when students from North Preston and Eastern Passage were first thrown together in the school in 1982, along with middle-class whites (and a smattering of equally middle-class blacks) from newly built suburban communities.

The whites and blacks of Preston and the Passage have been at each other's throats for a long time. How long has it been? Thirty years? Fifty years? One hundred years? Two hundred years? Were seeds planted in the distant past that continue to bear bitter fruit to this day?

That question needs to be answered before the long-term fate of the school is decided.

Headline-grabbing turmoil at Cole Harbour High has, unfortunately, become commonplace over the past year. There was the cafeteria fight in October 1996, and the Christmas dance brawl in December of that year. The school appeared to have quieted after that. Then, early in October, a fracas occurred that resulted in the suspensions of 13 students.

It was when parents of some suspended students brought their children to the school the next day for a confrontation with the administration that the community roots of the conflict became obvious. The subsequent mêlée, with parents threatening administrators, teachers and students, showed the source of the attitudes some students carry to school along with their lunches and backpacks.

Educators encourage parents to take an active role in their children's education — but not *that* active. The lessons some children learned from their parents' behavior on October 2 are detrimental.

By the way, great care has been taken not to reveal the racial identity of the parents of the suspended students. That omission illustrates the volatile state of race relations in the school. It's also a strong hint that some, if not all, of the parents were black, and their color is being obscured to prevent accusations of racism.

In the aftermath of the violence, Cole Harbour High was closed for a week while administration, teachers, parents and the school board struggled to find solutions. One was the adoption of the Blye Frank Report's recommendations, after the document had previously been shelved because of the costs its implementation would have incurred.

Extreme measures were proposed, such as closing the school and dispersing its 950 students among other Metro high schools. But that would have been an admission of defeat — and a victory for the terrorists, youth and adult, who have chosen to make the school their battleground.

The school finally opted to increase security, intensify its zero-tolerance policy (students will be suspended for violent or disrespectful behavior), expel persistent troublemakers and reopen in grade-by-grade stages.

For the most part, parents of all races and communities have approved the school's policies. But black parents have raised another problem.

Some parents have demanded the ouster of teachers they have accused of harassing and intimidating black students. They have also asked for the removal of administrators who are "part of the problem and not part of the solution."

This distrust among black parents is certain to collide with the zero-tolerance policy if the parents perceive that it is biased against their children. The parents' concerns are rooted in the 1989 Cole Harbour High violence, an incident that continues to cast a shadow even though the student body involved has long since departed. Although the brawls involved blacks and whites, only blacks were convicted. Whatever the legal reasons for that disparity might be, the outcome confirmed to many blacks that the system is stacked against them.

Those who implement the zero-tolerance policy need to take all possible measures to ensure that it is carried out fairly and not directed disproportionately against blacks. If equal justice at Cole Harbour High is not done and seen to be done; if blacks are once again the scapegoats, there will be zero tolerance for the school in the black community.

At a meeting of black parents last week, the possibility of a separate high school for North Preston students was raised. The fact that such a prospect was even mentioned is an indication of the gravity of black parents' concerns.

A separate school would be the last and worst resort. It would mean that all other alternatives had failed. It would mean the end of the dreams of several generations of blacks and whites alike — the dream that children of all races can be educated together so they can live in harmony as adults.

There is a precedent for such a withdrawal. Last year, when Mi'kmaq found conditions at East Hants High intolerable because of racism, they started their own educational institution. Not all the Mi'kmaq parents in the area pulled their children out of East Hants. But those who are attending the separate school appear adamant in their determination never to return to the scene of their misery.

A separate school was a step backward for the Mi'kmaq, and such a school would also be a step backward for blacks. Does anyone believe that separate ethnic schools would receive resources and facilities equal to those in the schools that were left behind, especially in the current era of budget cuts and teacher layoffs?

Still, there are times when it is necessary to step backward to avoid falling off a cliff. The Mi'kmaq saw an abyss at East Hants; blacks may see an abyss at Cole Harbour.

Hopefully, the zero-tolerance policy will work and the two solitudes of North Preston and Eastern Passage can learn to respect each other's right to send their children to a safe school. If that doesn't happen, and the collisions continue, the separation option will become difficult to avoid, and the challenge to provide equal educational opportunities for all students in the area will be abandoned.

And if it comes to that, then Cole Harbour High will have proven that it never deserved the privilege of the presence of North Preston's children.

There is, however, a ray of hope. Last Wednesday, more than 1,000 parents from both the white and black communities attended a meeting at the school to hear the new policies. In the past, meetings like that have featured verbal warfare between the two solitudes. This time, confrontation was at a minimum, and both sides seemed pleased with the outcome.

That's a first step. Perhaps the next one will be onto common ground.

Both Cole Harbour and Auburn Drive schools remained quiet through the end of the 1997/98 school year, as well as the beginning of 1998/99. Cole Harbour High operates under a strict regimen in which misbehavior is not tolerated and the school day ends not long after noon. Auburn Drive's rules are less stringent.

On the positive side, efforts are being made to bridge the racial divide in both schools. Especially noteworthy is an inter-racial school newspaper published at Cole Harbour.

If the violence of 1996 and '97 served as a wake-up call to school staff, students and parents, then the corner thought to have been turned in 1989 may finally, in fact, be turned by the year 2000.

Staff and students alike agree that the schools aren't yet out of the racial woods. However, efforts are being made to weed out the trouble-makers and build on a spirit of co-operation from all the communities from which the schools draw students.

Distraught observers leave court after sentences announced.
(Paul Darrow/The Daily News)

Fight at a frat house

A near-lethal beating puts justice on trial

In the fall of 1994, a party at a fraternity house near the campus of Dalhousie University turned into a near tragedy when a white fraternity brother, Darren Watts, was kicked and beaten into a coma by a group of young black men. Watts and two other fraternity brothers had intervened when a black man had a physical altercation with his white girlfriend outside the frat house.

Watts survived the beating and came out of his coma weeks later. As a result of his injuries, he suffered long-term brain damage.

Six black men, in their late teens and early 20s, were charged with aggravated assault against Watts and the others. A youth was also charged under the Young Offenders Act.

And in their ensuing odyssey through the legal system, their 1996 trial was only the beginning.

Dangerous mindsets
March 3, 1996

Anger and relief. Those are the emotions usually expressed when a high-profile criminal trial ends. So it was last Tuesday, when Nova Scotia Supreme Court Justice Jamie Saunders found six young black men guilty of attacking Darren Watts in the fall of 1994.

Two photos in that day's edition of *The Daily News* tell the story of the emotions this trial generated. One showed Watts's fraternity brothers in a group embrace. The other depicted one of the defendants, Stacey Skinner, undergoing a search while his glum-faced supporters look on.

Although racial tension lingered like a thundercloud over this trial, the circumstances were not entirely black-and-white. In the photo of Watts's fraternity brothers, one of the men in the group hug is black. And there is a white woman among the Skinner supporters.

The chain of events that led to the trial began innocently enough. In September, the start of the 1994-95 school year, Phi Kappa Pi fraternity held a party at its frat house on Robie Street. Terrance Dixon, a young black man, was there. His pregnant girlfriend, Shannon Burke, arrived to find him dancing with another woman. Burke attacked the woman, and Dixon dragged her out of the frat house.

Some of the fraternity brothers attempted to intervene as Dixon and Burke ended up among a group of Dixon's friends, who were black. Two of the fraternity brothers, both white, were punched by Dixon's friends.

Darren Watts, who is white, tried to help one of his brothers. He was knocked down, then kicked by the group of black men. The blacks then took off. Witnesses say they chanted, "We got to go and now you know" as they left the scene. A police officer was hit while trying to arrest one of the suspects.

Watts was taken to the hospital, where he lapsed into a coma. He underwent two brain operations, and required extensive rehabilitation after awakening from a coma that lasted two weeks.

A month after the attack, seven black men aged 18 to 24 were charged. At the trial, one of the suspects, Danny Clayton, testified against the others in exchange for immunity. His evidence played a major role in Saunders's decision to find all six defendants guilty of aggravated assault endangering the life of Watts and four guilty of separate charges of assault against the other two fraternity brothers.

Clayton admitted he had lied to police who were investigating the beating. However, Saunders said he "was not left with the sense that it would be unsafe to convict upon the testimony of Mr. Clayton."

Before Saunders was named to the bench in 1990, he represented the government during the Donald Marshall Inquiry. During the inquiry, he said that Marshall, who served 11 years in prison for a murder he did not commit, was partially to blame for his conviction because Marshall had "lied" to police about an attempted robbery. His standards on that issue appear to have changed since he became a judge.

After announcing his verdict, Saunders ordered the defendants jailed until their sentencing, a move that angered their supporters, not to mention their lawyers.

Race was a factor in the case from beginning to end. Terrance Dixon is black; Shannon Burke is white. The defendants were black; the victims were white. However, acknowledging that reality is not the same as accusing the police or the judicial system of racism.

Saunders addressed the race issue in his decision as follows: "I ... dismiss the notion that racism was a factor in these attacks ... (there) is not sufficient evidence for me to conclude that the men who encircled and beat Darren Watts were persuaded to do so because he is white and they are black. By the same token, I reject any assertion or inference that these six accused found themselves included as members of the group said to have attacked Darren Watts only because they were young, male, and black."

Saunders' statements attempted to defuse two racial time bombs. The first addressed the faddish tendency among some whites to accuse blacks and other minorities of racism. The second deals with the criminalization of young black males on both sides of the Canada-U.S. border.

The judge's effort was admirable, but not entirely successful. On the latter issue, opinion in the black community is split. Evangeline Cain-Grant, Stacey Skinner's lawyer, said racism was involved in the identification of the attackers and the trial was "racially charged." But activist-turned-lawyer Rocky Jones told Canadian Press it was "absolutely wrong" to portray the case as "just being a racial incident." Jones said it was symptomatic of a wider problem with youth in general.

In evaluating this latest encounter between blacks and the justice system, it is best to separate the trial from the crime. The judge based his convictions of the six defendants partly on the evidence of a perpetrator testifying under immunity, and partly on some of the defendants' admissions that they had hit Watts's two friends.

The defence lawyers pointed out doubts concerning Clayton's testimony. Saunders did not find those doubts reasonable, and he found the defendants guilty. Yet there will always be people who reasonably doubt the judge's verdict.

Let's not forget the crime, though. A large number of young men, some still in their teens, assaulted three others, stomping one within an inch of his life. Regardless of who the attackers were, or what color they were, their actions were deplorable and cannot be excused.

The outcome of the events that September night could have been much, much worse.

Darren Watts could have died, or suffered brain damage that would have impaired him the rest of his life.

Shannon Burke could have miscarried her child.

The whites at the party could have retaliated against the blacks, causing a riot on Robie Street.

The police officer who was knocked down while trying to make an arrest could have pulled his gun and shot at the suspects.

As Rocky Jones observed, the attack is evidence of a wider tendency, a nihilistic mindset among our youth. And beyond the youth, there is a backlash mindset that may prove just as destructive. Those mindsets could lead to the destruction not only of the black community, but civil society as we know it.

The mindset that says it's OK to attack another person because she is dancing with your boyfriend has got to end.

The mindset that says it's OK to physically assault the woman who is carrying your child has got to end.

The mindset that says it's OK to gang up on someone who hasn't done anything to you has got to end.

The mindset that says all young black men are suspects in the eyes of the law has got to end.

The mindset that says the police are not to be trusted under any circumstances has got to end.

How do we eliminate these mindsets? There is no easy answer. Hard thinking has to be done. Hard work has to be undertaken. Hard choices have to be made.

If we don't clean up our own act, someone else is going to do it for us, through vigilantism or an elected dictatorship — or both.

A week later, the judge sentenced the men he had convicted.

If Watts sentences fair, they set a new standard
March 10, 1996

Gasps of shock greeted the tough sentences Nova Scotia Supreme Court Justice Jamie Saunders imposed earlier this month on the six young black men he had earlier found guilty in the beatings of Darren Watts and two other Dalhousie University students at a fraternity party in September 1994.

The sentences, combined in some cases, totalled between seven and 10 years. Defence lawyers and supporters of the young men said the sentences were too harsh. Some of the defendants are planning to appeal their convictions and sentences.

But Saunders was apparently sending a message from the bench.

"People want their neighborhoods back," he told the defendants. "Whether they live on Robie and Cherry Streets or Gottingen and Creighton Streets, law-abiding citizens want to be able to walk about freely day and night without having to worry about criminals like you."

No reasonable person would disagree with that statement, although some might dispute the defendants' guilt. But was that the only message Saunders's sentencing imparted?

There are two ways to look at the severity of these sentences: in relation to the crime and in relation to previous cases.

In relation to the crime, the sentences would seem appropriate. Watts was punched and kicked viciously, and needed brain surgery and a long period of recovery. There is no need for him to have suffered such an assault.

However, a comparison between this case and others in the recent past raises disturbing questions.

147

After the trial, Evangeline Cain-Grant, one of the defence lawyers, said: "We've had people who have . . . killed in this province and have received less of a sentence."

She's right.

Consider the following:

The day before the sentences in the Watts beatings, Joseph Levy was given two years for beating his mother so badly that she spent the rest of her life — 11 months — in the hospital on life-support machines. Levy could have received five years, but was credited with the time he had spent in custody since his arrest for the assault in April 1994. Defence lawyers argued that Levy was in a drug-induced psychosis at the time of the attack.

Earlier in February, Reginald Brunt was sentenced to six years on a manslaughter charge for shooting Craig Gallant in the head during a struggle in a parking lot. Facing a trial for first-degree murder, Brunt pleaded guilty to the lesser charge. Three other men went free. Brunt had claimed self-defence because Gallant was reaching for a gun tucked in his pants.

Also in February, Gail McDow, who had been released from prison after serving four months of a two-year manslaughter sentence for the stabbing death of her common-law husband, was ordered back to prison when the Nova Scotia Court of Appeal increased her sentence to five years. The court rejected McDow's claim that she was an abused woman acting in self-defence.

Last November, Beatrice Whynot appealed a manslaughter sentence she was given for stabbing her husband to death in 1992. Originally charged with second-degree murder, she pleaded guilty to the lesser charge. The length of the sentence she is appealing: five years.

Also in November, John Boyd was sentenced to seven years in prison for manslaughter after stabbing another man to death in a fight. Boyd pleaded guilty to the lesser charge after an original charge of second-degree murder.

In 1994, Michael Power and his common-law wife, Cheryl Myers, pleaded guilty to manslaughter in the mercy-killing death of Myers' father, Layton. Judge Felix Cacchione said: "I find their actions, though illegal, done out of mercy, compassion and love." The couple was sentenced to three years probation and 150 hours of community service.

Each of these cases involves singular circumstances: self-defence, drugs, mercy-killing. In only one, though, did the convicted person receive a sentence that matched even the lowest meted to the defendants in the Watts beating.

Whatever the circumstances, the bottom line is that Darren Watts is alive, and all the victims in the above-cited cases are dead. But Watts' assailants received more prison time.

Also, like it or not, coincidence or not, the defendants in the Watts case were black and the defendants in the other cases were white.

Saunders may be signalling a break from the past with the sentences he handed down. He may be saying it's time to provide dire consequences for unacceptable behavior.

If that's true, then people who commit similar or worse crimes in the future should receive sentences similar to or harsher than the ones handed down in the Watts case.

And if that doesn't happen, the message will be that when blacks are convicted in court, they get two sentences: one for the crime and the other for their color.

All six of the convicted men appealed the verdict. And as time passed, the Watts beating continued to divide Nova Scotians along racial lines.

The litmus test
June 30, 1996

The six-to-10-year sentences Justice Jamie Saunders handed down to six young black men convicted in the beating of fraternity member Darren Watts and two others continue to reverberate in metro's white and black communities.

Indeed, reactions to those sentences have become something of a racial litmus test.

On September 11, 1994, the three fraternity brothers were assaulted during an altercation at a frat-house party. Two received relatively minor injuries; Watts was kicked into a life-threatening coma. The six men were convicted of aggravated assault.

Those who believe the defendants' sentences were excessive have been accused of being soft on crime and eager to give black defendants

149

the benefit of a doubt they don't deserve. And those who think the sentences were appropriate, or even too lenient, are charged with contributing to the racist demonization of the young black male. Both accusations are extreme and counterproductive. Events that occurred earlier this month illustrate that point.

On June 11, the Brothers Reaching Out Society (BROS) held a march in protest of the "excessive, unusual and harsh" sentences blacks tend to receive in the criminal justice system. The case of the Watts beating served as a focal point; the sentencing disparity phenomenon occurs not just in Nova Scotia but throughout North America.

The marchers were not asking the courts to extend special leniency to blacks convicted of felonies and misdemeanors. They were simply asking for fairness — equal time for similar crimes, without having additional time tacked on for no reason other than the color of their skin.

Estimates of the number of marchers range from 70 to 150. The march was peaceful and conciliatory. Some of the reactions to it were neither.

Daily News columnist Harry Flemming, in response to a column in which Stephen Kimber questioned the length of the sentences in the Watts beating, wrote: "On what can only be called attempted murder, we would have hooligans given Mulligans — miss once, you deserve a second shot."

That's not a Mulligan — it's malarkey. Neither Kimber, BROS nor anyone else is suggesting that the beaters get off scot-free, which is what a "Mulligan" implies. Critics of the sentences are merely wondering why six black men convicted of aggravated assault received more prison time than some white men and women convicted of manslaughter, a more serious crime. If Flemming is looking for "humbuggery," in sentencing, that's where he'll find it.

Kimber and BROS were also attacked by letter-writer B. Arden Stevens of Halifax. Stevens wrote: "I can understand the BROS trying to pervert justice, as they are a special-interest group with their own agenda."

This is BROS' agenda, as expressed in the group's motto: Reaching Out, Pitching In, Lifting Up, Giving Back. The group's purpose is community self-help. BROS chairman Steve Benton says the purpose of the march was to bring attention to sentencing disparities. Does this sound like an attempt to "pervert justice"?

Finally, it should be mentioned that the appeal of one of the men convicted in the beating, Damon Cole, was heard around the same time that BROS held its march. Cole's defence argued that the prosecution failed to disclose the statement of a witness who said Cole was on the opposite side of the street when the beating occurred.

If that witness turns out to be credible, Cole's conviction should be overturned. He deserves justice, as does Darren Watts. And that is neither a "humbug" nor a "perversion of justice."

By the end of 1996, and into the beginning of 1997, the appeal process bore surprising fruit.

Both sides still looking for justice in Watts beating
January 26, 1997

Although the beating of Darren Watts occurred 28 months ago, its after-effects linger in the lives of Watts, the six young black men convicted of the crime, and the black and white communities of metro.

Earlier this month, two out of three judges of the Nova Scotia Court of Appeal upheld the convictions and sentences of five of the young men on charges of aggravated assault. The seven-to-eight-year sentences were the stiffest yet on that charge, and exceeded other sentences that had been handed down on manslaughter charges.

However, the appeal-court judges did reduce the five men's sentences for assaulting a pair of Watts's fraternity brothers, Rob Gillis and John Charman, to three months from two years.

The sixth person charged in the assault, Damon Cole, had his conviction for the Watts beating overturned by three other appeal court judges last year. He is out on bail, and his retrial has been stayed by the prosecution.

The court's decision is neither cut-and-dried nor — pardon the expression — black and white.

Because Justice Nancy Bateman dissented from the majority ruling of Justices David Chipman and Ted Flinn, the appeals are automatically eligible to be heard by the Supreme Court of Canada. Lawyers for three of the men have said they'll continue their appeals; two others are still thinking about it.

Like Cole's, the appeals of Cyril Smith, Herman McQuaid, Spencer Dixon, Stacey Skinner, and Guy Robart were based on the contention that the Crown had failed to disclose a statement to police given by Terris Daye, who had attended the fraternity party at which the beating occurred.

Cole's lawyer, Craig Garson, argued that Daye's statement contradicted some of key witness Danny Clayton's testimony at the trial. Daye's information could have diminished Clayton's credibility, and its absence at the trial may have undermined Cole's defence.

Justices Ronald Puglsey, Gerald Freeman, and Elizabeth Roscoe agreed with Garson's argument and granted Cole a new trial. Lawyers for the others hoped the non-disclosure issue would unlock the prison gates for their clients as well.

But Justices Chipman and Flinn didn't see it that way. In their view, the five men's lawyers did not exercise "due diligence" in seeking out the statements of Daye and three other witnesses the Crown didn't call during the trial. And even if defence counsel had obtained Daye's information in time for the trial, that would not have affected the outcome because, according to Chipman, "there is nothing of significance in the statement. Overall, the statement is negative and evasive."

Bateman disagreed. In her dissent, she wrote: "It may be that upon a retrial, the Terris Daye statement is of no assistance to the appellant(s), however, that is not the determining factor here. There is enough information in that statement to have made it a potentially important resource in assisting with the preparation and presentation of the defence."

Bateman's opinion is milder than that of Pugsley in the Cole appeal, in which he wrote: "I conclude that the failure of the Crown to disclose these ... statements deprived Mr. Cole of an opportunity to present full answer and defence to both the Watts and Gillis charges; accordingly it cannot be said, with certainty, that Mr. Cole received a fair trial."

Still, Bateman's dissent, combined with Cole's successful appeal, indicates a 50-50 chance that the Supreme Court could rule in favor of the appeals. Assuming that all five of the others go the Supreme Court route, the Crown has said it will re-try the six men together if the high court upholds the appeals the provincial court rejected.

If that happens, the case could drag on for several more years, trailing its bitter and divisive baggage along the way.

Amid all the speculation and recrimination the case has generated among blacks and whites alike, a few key facts remain:

Darren Watts was punched and kicked into a life-threatening coma, and continues to suffer the effects of brain damage.

Although hundreds of people were at the scene of the fight, the prosecution had difficulty finding witnesses who could identify Watts's assailants.

The Crown's case was centred on the testimony of a participant who gave evidence in exchange for immunity from prosecution.

The sentences were the harshest yet for the offence of aggravated assault.

Since the convictions in the Watts beating, judges have continued to impose lighter sentences on whites who have committed worse crimes.

Darren Watts did not deserve the beating he received in September of 1994. He does deserve justice. The only way he can get justice is if the right people are convicted of the crime and appropriate sentences are handed down.

So far, in two appeals, four of six judges have found fault with the conviction and sentencing of the men charged in the Watts beating. These young black men deserve justice, too. In that matter, the jury is still out.

The appeals process continued, with mixed results.

Watts beating retrials may not lead to closure
February 22, 1998

The aftermath of the Darren Watts beating case lingers long after the event occurred in the fall of 1994. In the latest twist of the tale, the Supreme Court of Canada has ordered a new trial for one of the six young black men convicted of beating and kicking Watts into a coma during a frat-house party and assaulting two other fraternity members, who attempted to intervene in an altercation between a black man and a white woman.

Watts has since recovered and is now the Liberal MLA candidate for the Halifax Atlantic riding.

The six defendants were given sentences of seven to 10 years for aggravated assault — the harshest yet issued for that offence. Several people have received lighter sentences for manslaughter. All six appealed their convictions.

The appeal of one, Damon Cole, reached the Nova Scotia Court of Appeal in 1996. The court ordered a new trial because the Crown had not disclosed the statement of a witness, Terris Daye, which could have been helpful to the defence.

The Daye statement was also the basis for the other appeals.

The Crown decided to postpone Cole's retrial until the appeals of the other five men had been heard.

Now, the result of those appeals is in.

One of the men, Stacey Skinner, has won the right to a new trial for the Watts beating on the same grounds that formed the basis of Cole's appeal. He is free on bail, as is Cole.

Cyril Smith's conviction for the Watts beating was upheld, but the judges ordered a new trial for the assault of one of the other fraternity brothers.

The convictions of the other three men — Spencer Dixon, Herman McQuaid and Guy Robart — were upheld because the judges didn't think Daye's statement could have helped them.

Thus far, the reversal of two of the Watts beating convictions has not stirred up a public outcry. But if Cole and Skinner are acquitted on retrial, certain segments of the population could erupt in anger. Such a reaction would be a replay of attitudes prevalent at the time of the beating and the first trial.

Back then, young black men were regarded as the number one menace to society. In the public's perception, the face of crime had long since become black, and the fact that lawbreakers come in all colors was ignored.

Although the trial judge, Justice Jamie Saunders, took great pains to distance himself from the race issue in his sentencing, the words he used were all too familiar: "People want their neighborhoods back. Whether they live on Robie and Cherry Streets or Gottingen and Creighton Streets, law-abiding citizens want to be able to walk about freely day and night without having to worry about criminals like you."

"Criminals like you" could easily be interpreted as an allusion to the race of the defendants. Again, Saunders may not have meant any racial connotation.

But for the racially intolerant, the implication was clear: Get rid of young black males and the streets will be safer for young white males.

That was two years ago — a short time, but long enough for circumstances and attitudes to alter.

The Watts beating and subsequent trial occurred before other high-profile racial incidents such as the fights at Cole Harbour and Auburn Drive High Schools and the standoff between blacks and police in North Preston. Also, misdeeds involving non-blacks have served to lighten the face of crime in the public eye.

Still, new trials for Cole and Skinner could reopen old wounds. Cole may not even have to face trial again. His lawyer is seeking to have his case dismissed on the grounds that his right to a speedy trial has been compromised. If the Cole case doesn't make it to trial, the "lock-'em-up-and-throw-away-the-key" crowd will yell long and loud.

The outcome of a new trial — or trials — will hinge on a "he-said-he-said" scenario.

In the first trial, the key witness was Danny Clayton, who admitted to participating in the beating of Watts. Clayton testified against the others in exchange for immunity from prosecution. It was his identification of the six defendants that convinced Saunders of their guilt. (The defendants had chosen to be tried by a judge instead of a jury.) Although defence lawyers attacked Clayton's credibility, the judge believed him.

A second trial will pit Clayton's credibility against Daye's. In the current climate of attack lawyering, it's a foregone conclusion that the Crown will try to crucify Daye on the witness stand.

The judge might have difficulty deciding which story to believe, and the two witnesses could therefore cancel each other out, which would open the door to reasonable doubt.

Such an outcome would be far from satisfying, either to Watts or the defendants, who would forever be considered by some to have gotten off on a technicality.

Still, the case cries out for justice. The beating of Watts was a terrible crime, regardless of the color of his attackers. Those attackers deserve stiff punishment. But all defendants deserve a fair trial, regardless of the color of the victim.

In the middle of 1998, the Watts beating case came closer to a discordant end.

Not with a bang but a whimper
May 10, 1998

The Darren Watts case, which began with a brutal beating at a fraternity house in the fall of 1994, has reached the final stage of an inconclusive, unsatisfying end.

On Wednesday, Nova Scotia Supreme Court Justice Suzanne Hood granted a judicial stay to Damon Cole, one of six young black men who were convicted of beating and kicking Watts into a coma and assaulting two other men during a party at Watts's fraternity house. Watts and the others had intervened in an altercation between one of the black men and his girlfriend.

The stay means Cole cannot be retried on charges of aggravated assault, and is free after serving six months of an eight-year prison sentence.

Cole appealed the original 1996 verdict and sentence, as did the other five men, on the grounds that the Crown had failed to disclose the statement of witness Terris Daye, which could have helped in their defence.

Later in 1996, the Nova Scotia Court of Appeal overturned Cole's conviction. And earlier this year, the Supreme Court of Canada ordered a new trial for Stacey Skinner for the Watts beating. Also, Cyril Smith was awarded a new trial for the assault of one of the other fraternity brothers. His conviction for the Watts beating was upheld.

The convictions of the other three men, Spencer Dixon, Herman McQuaid, and Guy Robart, were upheld. They continue to serve the longest prison terms a Nova Scotia court has yet imposed for aggravated assault charges, sentences longer than other people have received for manslaughter.

Hood ruled that the Crown's decision to stay the charges against Cole after the Supreme Court quashed his conviction, then re-lay them many months later, was an abuse of power.

"The court made no decision and Damon Cole had no say," Hood said. "There was no appeal process . . . I conclude that this is one of those clear cases for granting a stay."

Prosecutors argued that they had delayed Cole's retrial pending the outcomes of the other men's appeals, so that everyone whose conviction was overturned could be retried at the same time, thus saving the time and complications that would have been involved in multiple trials. The judge disagreed, saying the Crown should have begun a retrial of Cole, then asked for an adjournment pending the other appeals.

That's a legal technicality. Hood's ruling doesn't shed any light on Cole's guilt or innocence. And so, even though he won't be spending any more time in jail, Cole has not really been vindicated. Only a not-guilty verdict in a new trial would have provided that satisfaction. However, the ruling is yet another slap in the face of the Crown, which has suffered more than a few setbacks over the past few years.

A retrial would have pitted the testimony of Daye against that of the prosecution's star witness, Danny Clayton. In the 1996 trial, Clayton had testified in exchange for immunity against prosecution. He identified the six men, and a young offender, as the culprits in the beating. Without Clayton's testimony, the judge might not have convicted Cole or Skinner.

In a second trial, Daye's testimony would have contradicted Clayton's, and the verdict would have hinged on which witness's testimony was more consistent and believable. Perhaps the judge would have believed one over the other. Perhaps the two stories would have cancelled each other out. We'll never know, unless the Crown decides to appeal Hood's ruling and succeeds in forcing another trial. That decision is expected this week.

So in the end, Cole is free, but not acquitted. Skinner is still awaiting the Crown's decision on whether or not to re-try him. Clayton may not be available to testify in a retrial. He is under psychiatric care in Toronto, and reports indicate his caregivers are recommending against another trip to the witness stand.

The Crown will not retry Smith because he has already served his time for the lesser charge. The other three men will probably be out of prison sometime next year if they win parole. And the Crown could appeal Hood's decision.

A case that began as a racially charged melodrama has ended in ambivalence. After weeks in a coma, Watts recovered sufficiently to run (unsuccessfully) for the Liberals in the recent provincial election. But one more kick to the head might have killed him, and he still suffers side effects from his injuries.

The passions that surrounded the circumstances of the beating and the trial have cooled over the past four years. Any lessons that may have been learned have long since been absorbed, or forgotten, or ignored.

Hopefully, the most lasting lesson will be that if the legal system is flawed or racially biased, quick fixes will not work.

Like the Watts beating's courtroom chronicle, the quest to ensure that justice is done and seen to be done will be long, hard and occasionally painful.

Justice delayed yet again in Watts case
May 24, 1998

In the matter of the Darren Watts beating, the wheels of justice continue to grind slowly, and not particularly fine.

Stacy Skinner, whose conviction for aggravated assault in a 1994 attack that left Watts in a coma for weeks was quashed by the Supreme Court of Canada, was told he must wait another six weeks before he learns whether or not he will face a retrial.

Like Damon Cole, another of the six men convicted for the beating, Skinner received the benefit of the highest court's doubt because the Crown failed to disclose a statement by a witness that might have helped the defence. Cole's case was stayed by a Nova Scotia Supreme Court judge. But Skinner remains in legal limbo.

Part of Skinner's problem is that he has been unable to obtain legal representation. Again and again, he goes to court, tells the judge he has no lawyer, and is told to find one before he comes back. The decision in the Cole case, which was based on delays in scheduling his retrial, could have had a bearing on whether or not Skinner would also face another trial.

Last week, however, the Crown stated that it could not begin a retrial against Skinner because the prosecution's star witness, Danny Clayton, is suffering a psychological disorder.

However, the long story of the Watts beating is drawing to a close, fitful though it may be. The Crown has stated that it will not retry Skinner if Clayton is still unable to testify at the time of the next court date, June 18.

If that happens, and the Crown decides not to appeal the judge's ruling in Cole's case, the legal system aftermath of the Watts beating will finally end. If not, it could drag on for another year or more; trying not only the defendants, but also the patience of the public.

In June, the Crown announced it would not pursue a retrial of Skinner because its star witness, Danny Clayton, would not testify.

Senator Calvin Ruck greets beauty queen Tamara Tynes at the 15th anniversary celebration of the Black Cultural Centre for Nova Scotia. *(Darrell Oake/The Daily News)*

Milestones

History remembered, history made

The history of Nova Scotia's black community is long, and has long been overlooked by the province as a whole. However, efforts have been made to honor that past, and to recognize history in the making as well. These are some of the milestones of African-Nova Scotian history from the perspective of the 1990s.

Uncrowned champion
June 14, 1992

On June 6, the government of Canada paid tribute to one of Nova Scotia's greatest heroes: Sam Langford, who has gone down in history as the greatest boxer never to hold a world championship.

Langford was born 106 years ago in Weymouth Falls, a historically black community in Digby County. It was therefore fitting that the Historic Sites and Monuments Board of Canada has installed a new plaque and permanent exhibit in Langford's honor at the Weymouth Falls Community Centre that bears his name.

Despite rains that bordered on the torrential, the centre was packed with people who had come from across the province and country to witness the dedication of the memorial.

I had the honor of being one of the speakers that day, sharing the platform with Historic Sites Chairman Thomas H.B. Symons, Nova Scotia Education Minister Guy Leblanc, Senator Donald Oliver, and Joseph Jarvis of the Weymouth Falls Community Council. Also present were three of Langford's oldest living relatives: a niece, Mrs. Bernice Beals, and two cousins, George and James Langford.

Despite the wet weather and crowded conditions caused by a turnout that exceeded the organizers' most optimistic dreams, the event generated a tremendous amount of positive energy. Black or white, old or young, rich or poor — everyone shared in the homage that was Langford's just due.

In and out of the ring, Sam Langford's exploits can be summed up in a single word: extraordinary. When he ran away from home as a youngster and made his way to Boston, he began a career that took him around the world, and eventually landed him in boxing's Hall of Fame.

It's difficult for us today to imagine Sam Langford's world: the world of this century's first 20 years. Basic human rights we take for granted today were only a dream back then. Black people's aspirations crashed daily against a wall built of intolerance and indifference.

Yet blacks struggled to shatter that wall, brick by brick. Some battles were small, others large and sweeping. The most spectacular and visible of those battles were fought within the confines of the boxing ring.

It was in the brutal profession of pugilism that blacks first competed successfully with whites to achieve world-wide respect and renown. Through a sport that stressed elemental one-on-one combat, black fighters gradually earned an admiration that was both grudging and sincere.

The early black boxers were giants in their field. They had to be. George Dixon of Africville was the first. Then came Barbados Joe Walcott, Joe Gans, Dixie Kid, Jack Johnson . . . all pioneer black champions. And even though he never got the opportunity to fight for a title, Sam Langford's name belongs in that elite company. It only stands to reason — he beat most of them, and the others wouldn't fight him.

Langford stood 5'7" and weighed 135 pounds when he began boxing as a teenager. He built himself up to 170 rock-hard pounds in his prime, and he consistently flattened opponents twice his size. In his most important fight, on April 26, 1906, Langford lost a 15-round decision to heavyweight Jack Johnson. Although the then-150-pound Langford was dwarfed by Johnson's six-foot, 185-pound physique, the bout was closely contested.

Two years later, Johnson became the first black fighter to win the heavyweight championship of the world. Despite Langford's persistent efforts, Johnson refused to give him a title shot. Perhaps those 20 extra pounds Sam added to his frame were more than Johnson could handle.

Throughout the rest of his career, which spanned more than 20 years and nearly 300 recorded bouts, Langford had to be content with the title "Uncrowned Champion."

Langford brought more than mere brute force into the ring. He brought keen wit as well. Here's an example. Once, when Sam fought in England, a sportswriter tried to bait him, saying: "Mr. Langford, your opponent is a very intelligent man, thinking every moment in the ring. How do you propose to cope with that?" Langford replied: "While he's thinking, I'll be hitting him."

Outside the ring, Langford battled racism in his own way. A 1910 newspaper story excerpted below provides one example: "For the first time in 20 years, according to followers of southern boxing, a colored fighter applied for accommodations at a first-class hotel in Memphis and was refused. Sam Langford, the Boston negro, who arrived for matches there had his first experience in the south of this kind, but made no demonstration. Several hundred negroes met Langford at the station and scores of pickaninnies followed him when he started training in eight inches of snow."

That same year, Langford "integrated" a Pullman sleeping car on a train travelling through Kentucky. The railway company was later indicted by a Paducah, Ky. grand jury for violating the state's segregation laws. Within the context of the rampant racism of that era, those were acts of considerable courage on Langford's part.

Langford's courage and sense of humor carried him through adverse times after he hung up his gloves. Because he fought well past his prime, he took punches that eventually rendered him blind. Yet when a sportswriter named Al Laney found him living penniless in a Harlem tenement in 1944, Langford said: "Don't nobody need to feel sorry for old Sam."

Because of Laney's subsequent story on Langford, a pension was established that supported Sam until his death in 1956. Sixteen years later, the people of Weymouth Falls honored him with a plaque of their own that is now part of the Historic Sites exhibit.

Finally — about that downpour at the ceremony. Could that have been Jack Johnson, once again trying to rain on Sam's parade? If so, it didn't work.

Proud day:
Feds to honor black battalion
January 17, 1993

July 10, 1993. Mark that date on your calendar. That's when the No. 2 Construction Battalion, the first and only black unit formed by the Canadian armed forces, will receive official recognition from the Historic Sites and Monuments Board of Canada.

The No. 2 Construction Battalion was created in 1916 during the First World War, which lasted from 1914 to 1918. Although the purpose of the Allied forces was to "make the world safe for democracy," most black Canadians who volunteered to serve their country found the door to the military slammed shut by segregation. Usually, black volunteers received two standard reasons for their rejection: (1) White troops would refuse to fight alongside black trenchmates, and (2) Blacks allegedly lacked the necessities to become good soldiers. When the excuses ran out, they were simply told it was a "white man's war."

Those attitudes prevailed despite plenty of historical evidence to the contrary. Black soldiers had fought for Canada in the War of 1812 and the Rebellion of 1837, and a black Nova Scotian, William Hall, had received the Victoria Cross.

Under persistent pressure from young black men who were determined to fight for the right to fight for their country, the Canadian military finally authorized the recruitment of an all-black non-combatant labor unit. Eventually, 605 men were accepted into the battalion. They came from all parts of Canada as well as the United States. Half the recruits were Nova Scotians, and a look at the roster reveals many old Nova Scotian black family names: Elms, Cromwell, Downey, Farmer, Paris, Marsman, Carvery, Bundy, Tynes.

On March 28, 1917, the battalion sailed to England on the *S.S. Southland*. Their commander was Lieutenant-Colonel. D.H. Sutherland of River John, Nova Scotia and Honorary Captain William A. White served as their chaplain. White was the only black commissioned officer in the British forces during the First World War.

The unit served honorably in France, working with the Forestry Corps to provide lumber necessary to maintain trenches on the front lines. Some of its members went on to serve in combat units. The battalion was disbanded in 1920, and seemed destined to fade into the mists of time, overlooked by the history books.

However, the veterans of the unit and their families never forgot. And one man became determined to revive the memory of the No. 2 Construction Battalion.

In 1982 Calvin W. Ruck, a social worker and civil servant from Sydney, helped to organize a reunion of the surviving veterans of the unit at the Lord Nelson Hotel in Halifax.

Four years later, Ruck published a book called *Canada's Black Battalion*, a history of the unit. The book contained a wealth of anecdotal and documentary material that told the story of brave men who refused to accept rejection.

As former battalion member Gordon Charles Wilson told Ruck, "Black people refused to accept the attitude that it was a white man's war. As loyal citizens, we wanted to serve our country. It was our duty, our responsibility."

While doing his research for the book, Ruck noticed that there was no marker or monument at the battalion's original headquarters — the Market Wharf in Pictou.

"There was nothing there to indicate to tourists or anyone else that this site has historical significance," Ruck says.

In 1987, Ruck approached Ernest Jordan, who was then mayor of Pictou, and suggested that the Market Wharf receive recognition for its role in Canadian history. Jordan agreed enthusiastically. Four years later, Pictou town council declared the site a municipal historic property. Ruck says the level of cooperation in Pictou was outstanding.

From there, the Pictou Council and the Black Cultural Centre for Nova Scotia mounted a joint effort to gain national recognition for the site and the battalion. The Centre established a Black Battalion Memorial Committee with Ruck serving as chairman. Other committee members included Wayne Adams, Douglas and Florence Bauld, Henry Bishop, George Borden, Irvine Carvery, Francis Dorrington, Doris Evans, and Anne Simmons.

The effort achieved success last month when federal Public Works Minister Elmer MacKay announced the Historic Sites and Monuments Board's decision to commemorate the Market Wharf for its role as headquarters for the No. 2 Construction Battalion. A plaque and display will be unveiled on July 10.

This is the second consecutive year that the Historic Sites Board has honored the contributions of black Nova Scotians. In June 1992 boxer Sam Langford was commemorated in Weymouth Falls.

Hopefully, the turnout at the July 10 ceremony will reflect the high esteem in which the No. 2 Construction Battalion is held by Nova Scotians of all colors.

N.S. has link to Sierra Leone
April 10, 1994

Geographically, Nova Scotia and Sierra Leone are far apart, separated by the Atlantic Ocean. History, however, is another matter. A common thread of ancestry ties the Canadian province to the West African nation. And that connection is about to be renewed as Haligonian Wayn Hamilton begins a two-year stint in Sierra Leone as a Regional Co-operant Assistant for Canadian University Services Overseas (CUSO).

"My job will be to find out and address specific developmental needs in Sierra Leone," Hamilton said shortly before departing. "I'll be concentrating on women and youth."

This will be Hamilton's third trip to Sierra Leone. On his second trip, two years ago, he discovered another branch of his family in Freetown, Sierra Leone's capital.

The division of those branches occurred more than 200 years ago, when a large group of Black Loyalists who had migrated to Nova Scotia after the American Revolution set sail for Sierra Leone, which was then a British colony set aside for freed slaves. One side of the Hamilton family boarded the ships that left Halifax harbour; the other remained in Nova Scotia.

The Loyalists were but one of several black immigrant groups that joined with the indigenous African people to create a new nation. In 1787 the British settled more than 300 destitute blacks from England in Freetown. The British blacks, called the Black Poor, were ex-slaves freed by a court decision that abolished slavery on British — but not colonial — soil.

Five years later, the Black Loyalists arrived from Nova Scotia. In 1800 the third immigrant group arrived — the Maroons, freedom fighters from Jamaica who came by way of Nova Scotia.

The final group of immigrants was the Recaptives, who were Africans rescued from slave ships by the British Navy after 1807, when Parliament abolished the Atlantic slave trade. Previously, the British had been avid participants in that trade. Now their warships intercepted slave ships and resettled the captives in Sierra Leone. The Recaptives, who came to number in the tens of thousands, came from many places in West Africa, but remained in Sierra Leone to avoid the risk of re-enslavement in their home countries.

Eventually, the immigrants' bloodlines mingled to create a community called the Krio, from "Creole," a word that originally referred to people of French ancestry who were born in Louisiana.

"The Krios can still trace their roots through their names," says Hamilton. "When the Hamiltons there heard my name and learned I was from Nova Scotia, they accepted me as family."

Throughout the rest of the 19th century, the Krios dominated the area around Freetown. A variety of indigenous ethnic groups — the Temne, Mende, Limba, Vai, and others — held the interior of the country. Because of rebellions against taxes and other manifestations of colonial rule, the British in 1896 divided Sierra Leone into two parts: the Crown Colony, which was Freetown, and the Protectorate, which was the interior.

When the British dismantled their colonial empire after the Second World War, the two parts of Sierra Leone were reunited, with the numerically superior indigenous people gaining power at the Krios' expense. Although ethnic disputes continue, the Sierra Leone government has remained remarkably stable since the country became independent in 1961.

This stability contrasts sharply with the situation in neighboring Liberia. Like Sierra Leone, Liberia was founded as a haven for freed slaves. Liberia's sponsor was the United States. Also like Sierra Leone, Liberia developed its own "Krio" class called "Americo-Liberians."

Unlike Sierra Leone, Liberia's ethnic conflicts exploded into brutal warfare, and conditions in that country today are hellish. Sierra Leone's leaders are looking over their shoulders at Liberia and are doing what they can to avoid that country's grim future.

In the meantime, Wayn Hamilton will work to forge closer links between Sierra Leone and Nova Scotia.

"They are eager to connect," he says. "They have a strong interest in the African diaspora."

North Preston lawyer "breaking down barriers"
August 21, 1994

This Saturday, North Preston will honor Evangeline Cain-Grant, the first person from that community to become a lawyer, graduating from Dalhousie University Law School earlier this year.

Sponsors of the event include the North Preston Ratepayers Association, the Parent-Student Association of Preston (PSAP) and Cain-Grant's family.

Of Cain-Grant's achievement, PSAP Chairwoman Madeline Downey says: "I believe that this event symbolizes the breaking down of barriers for black women in Nova Scotia."

The widely publicized racial brawls at Cole Harbour District High School in 1989 marked a turning point in Cain-Grant's life. In the wake of what was considered an unfair prosecution of black youths involved in the fights, she became the founding president of PSAP. The Cole Harbour incident wound its way through the courts for several years, ending when the provincial Supreme Court upheld the convictions of two young black men.

The experience taught Cain-Grant an important lesson.

"The law has been one of the most oppressive tools used against us. But it's a tool we can use to help ourselves as a community once we understand it," she says.

Cain-Grant then decided to study law at Dalhousie under the Indigenous Black and Mi'kmaq Program, which had been instituted to bring more black and native lawyers into the system. She was accepted into the program as a mature student.

"I found it challenging, but not surprising," she says. "I had to conform to the dominant system without losing myself at the same time. Through it all, I realized that I had to find a way of including my community's perspective and reality while I was learning the dominant community's perspective."

Sometimes, the dominant community's perspective posed difficulties.

"There were problems with some professors and some non-IBM students," Cain-Grant recalls. "Some of them had negative attitudes and stereotypes about black people. I coped by remaining silent most of the time. I had my own agenda, and wasn't going to let their attitudes stand in my way. It cost me in terms of pain and heartache to allow racist attitudes to flourish. But I didn't have the time and energy to finish law school and change people's attitudes."

Those attitudes included the perception that the IBM program is an example of affirmative action. And, due to distortions and downright lies spread by the reactionary right, affirmative action has become the political whipping-boy of the '90s.

Cain-Grant prefers to use the phrase "access programs" rather than "affirmative action." Terminology aside, her defence of the IBM program and others like it is vigorous.

"Some of the most biting criticism I've faced is the belief that access programs are unfair; that they are reverse discrimination; that recipients should feel it demeaning to benefit from them," she says.

"My position is, why should we feel demeaned when for generations we were denied access to education and employment opportunity? Now that those opportunities are here, there is no need to feel ashamed to accept them. I, for one, am proud to say, 'Yes, I am a recipient of an access program.'"

Cain-Grant was called to the bar on June 17, having passed the same bar examination all the other candidates were required to write. There's no such thing as an affirmative-action bar exam. Regardless of how she got into law school, the qualifications Cain-Grant and other IBM graduates possess are the same as those of any other Dal Law graduate.

Cain-Grant intends to begin her own law practice in Halifax next month. She has also been appointed as a *per diem* Crown prosecutor, which means she will handle surplus Crown cases.

She looks forward to the challenges her new career offers.

"It's important to have good, strong, skilled leadership to struggle for justice and equality in a society that devalues or doesn't appreciate certain segments.

"I'm happy to be recognized as the first lawyer from North Preston — the first of many more to come."

United and divided
February 4, 1996

Late last month, the Black United Front closed the doors of its Halifax head office and five regional branches because of financial difficulties. BUF is saddled with a $99,541 shortfall from this year's budget, and the Department of Community Services has refused to guarantee the organization's funding for the next fiscal year.

If the shutdown of BUF is indeed permanent, its collapse may appear to be abrupt. However, the organization has been living on borrowed time since its inception in November 1968, when 400 black Nova Scotians gathered at the North Branch Library in the wake of a visit to Halifax by members of the notorious Black Panther Party.

Although 27 years and a few months is a respectable amount of time to borrow, the fate of BUF was sealed less than a year after that momentous meeting. That was when the infant organization received grants totalling more than $500,000 over a five-year period from the federal government.

Fear, not altruism, motivated that initial funding. In his book *Beneath the Clouds of the Promised Land*, Bridglal Pachai provides this quote from a June 16, 1969, Cabinet Committee on Social Policy and Cultural Affairs memorandum: "There was a possibility of violence in the black community of Nova Scotia and a possible disruption of the Canadian Games this summer by black militants. A grant now might alleviate this situation. Absence of support might enable black militants to take over from the moderates now in charge of the Black United Front . . ."

Fears of a Nova Scotian counterpart to the black riots that wracked the U.S. during the 1960s soon subsided. But funding for BUF continued, with provincial coffers substituting for those of the federal government. Recently, almost all of BUF's funding has come from the Department of Community Services.

Still, what governments give, governments can take away. Ask Devco. Ask Sysco. Ask Via Rail.

And now, ask BUF.

Where does BUF go from here? Does it pass quietly into history, to be preceded from now on with the words "the defunct"? Or does the organization reinvent itself?

At this point, BUF leaders are attempting to maintain the group's status quo by persuading Community Services Minister Jim Smith to restore provincial funding. BUF Council president Eddie Parris told *The Daily News*: "The government's mind can be changed."

But Smith appears intransigent, indeed, even hostile to funding BUF. After the shutdown was announced, Smith said: "You have to question whether they do have broad support in the black community. Why can't they get an alternate source of funding?"

Smith may be Community Affairs minister, but he seems abysmally ignorant about black community affairs. With unemployment in some black areas exceeding 50 per cent, exactly where does Smith think "alternate" funding is supposed to come from? Piggybanks full of pennies?

Smith's "relevance" and "support" questions are less straightforward. A look at BUF's history might provide some answers.

Back in 1969, BUF was intended to be an "umbrella" organization under which other groups would gather to fight for the common cause of racial justice.

That intention was not fulfilled. The problem with umbrella groups is that the people under the umbrella tend to argue over who gets to hold the handle. BUF was no exception to that tendency. BUF did not become a group that supersedes all others; it is just one of many black organizations that are often in competition for funding and loyalty.

The "umbrella" goal was, perhaps, doomed from BUF's beginning. But there are still useful purposes the group could — and does — serve.

"Advocacy" is the word most often used to describe what BUF does. At the community level, BUF workers provide practical, one-on-one services that include race-relations mediation, employment counselling, and legal assistance. This work is seldom, if ever, reported in the media. Generally, the only time BUF makes the news is when the group suffers internal dissent or financial problems. BUF's unfavorable media image is part of a climate that allows the government to pull the funding plug without having to worry very much about possible accusations of racism.

However, BUF has also been characterized as a political organization — not a party such as the Tories, Grits, and NDP; but a voice with a mandate to speak out against racism wherever it occurs, even in the government that provides the group's funds. The conflict between BUF's mandate and the source of its money has weakened the considerable political clout the group enjoyed during its early years.

Smith has said money previously set aside for BUF in his department's budget will be distributed elsewhere in the black community. He plans to talk with black community groups to determine how the pie is to be sliced. BUF, of course, will get nothing.

This tactic is blatantly divisive. The inevitable battle among black organizations to get a share of BUF's money will create bitterness within the black community that will last at least 27 more years.

BUF has to decide once and for all what it wants to be. If the group wants to be a government-funded social-service provider, then it should drop all pretences of political advocacy and become part of the bureaucracy. And it should also drop its name, which would under those circumstances be a misnomer.

On the other hand, if BUF wants to be a political pressure group, it should divorce itself from the provincial government. The organization would then need to rely on the black community's limited resources for its survival. But at least it would no longer be subjected to the whims of government cost-cutters.

Despite its accomplishments over three decades, BUF has tried to be all things to all people, and in the process became divided against itself. That division led to BUF's downfall.

Although the community services department will determine BUF's immediate future, its long-term fate is in the hands of the black community — and, perhaps, piggybanks full of pennies.

Not just history
October 13, 1996

This week, the Nova Scotia Home for Colored Children celebrates its 75th anniversary. The focus of the commemoration is a conference called Black Family Focus: Year 2000, which will be held at the Westin Nova Scotian Hotel. Other events include an original stage play based on the home's history and a banquet featuring guest speaker Clifton Davis. An actor and a minister, Davis is best known for his starring roles in the TV sitcoms *Amen* and *That's My Mama*. He is now Vice-Chancellor for development and planning at Elizabeth City State University in North Carolina.

Davis is no stranger to Nova Scotia. His father, Rev. T.L. Davis, once served as pastor for the Hammonds Plains United Baptist Church.

Since its inception, the home has been an important part of this province's history. During its official opening day on June 6, 1921, a crowd of 3,000 — blacks and whites alike — gathered for day-long ceremonies that included speeches by the then-Lieutenant-Governor, the Premier and ministers from several denominations.

One of the home's founders, J.A.R. Kinney, called that day "the greatest event in the history of the colored people of Nova Scotia." And so it was.

The institution was created in response to a pressing necessity. During the early years of this century, racial segregation pervaded all aspects of society, including the care of children orphaned or abandoned by their families. Black children in need of care were routinely turned away from white institutions.

The black leaders of the time, including Kinney and lawyer James R. Johnston, proposed the development of a separate institution to accommodate the needs of black children. The white establishment embraced that idea, and worked with black groups, especially the African United Baptist Association, to turn the dream into a reality in 1921.

Because the home was the only black orphanage in Canada, it served the needs of hundreds of children from across the country and in some cases nearby U.S. states. Still, most of the home's residents were from Nova Scotia. The home also employed people from the Halifax-Dartmouth area as child-care workers and in its school and farm.

Times changed, and so did the circumstances of the home. The segregation that led to its founding began to ease in the 1960s. As well, social-service authorities decided that group homes and foster care for needy children were preferable to large orphanages.

The home adapted to those changes. Not only is this the 75th anniversary of the opening of the original home, it's also the 16th anniversary of its move to the two new buildings in which it is now located. The old home remains intact, but unused.

More than just the location of the home changed in 1978. Its direction changed as well. Instead of an orphanage, it became a group home for troubled children. Instead of an all-black institution, it became integrated. And the group and foster homes that replaced previously all-white institutions became integrated as well.

The home began to take in a small number of white children in the mid-1960s. Today, the majority of the home's residents are white. The home's staff, once virtually all-black, is now integrated. So is its board of directors, which was mostly white at the time of its founding.

The home is thus an example of two-way integration as opposed to the one-way variety. In one-way integration, minorities abandon their own institutions in an attempt to assimilate with those of the majority. But if the process of assimilation isn't successful, the minority is left with nothing to fall back on.

In two-way integration, the minority's institutions become open to the majority, and vice-versa. Each group's institutions retain their identity, but broaden their scope and become more inclusive. That's the road the home has wisely and successfully taken since the mid-1980s.

Even so, it could be argued that because the rigid segregation that prevailed at the time of its founding no longer exists, there is no longer any need for a Nova Scotia Home for Colored Children. But it's more to the point to argue that the nature of the need has changed.

Segregation is gone, but racism remains. Black children continue to suffer from its effects, and the home is an important resource for the alleviation of that suffering. Currently, it fulfills that need in conjunction with, rather than separate from, the rest of the social-services system.

The home may be 75 years old, but it's not just history.

The theme of the conference, Black Families in Focus: Year 2000, indicates that the home will continue to be part of our future.

Sparky Paris:
A gentleman and a fighter
August 31, 1997

Once upon a time, you didn't need to have cable TV to watch boxing. You didn't have to hope the major networks would televise a fight once in a blue moon. You didn't have to search the TV listings to find out when TSN shows month-old reruns of important fights. You didn't have to pay almost $70 to watch one fighter try to bite another's ear off. You didn't have to witness professional boxing degenerate into a comedy of errors.

In that earlier time, boxing was as close as the nearest arena — and there were plenty of arenas. The fighters didn't get paid much, but they fought often, plying a circuit of small clubs throughout the Maritimes. Boxing belonged to the fighters back then, not the big-time promoters and media moguls.

Those of us born in the baby-boom generation were children during the tail-end of that time, and for later generations it exists only in books or yellowed newspaper clippings or stories told by grandparents.

It was Hugh "Sparky" Paris' time. As a boxer and trainer, Paris was part of the events chronicled in those anecdotes and articles.

This Saturday, Paris's family will be honoring his 75th birthday in his home town, New Glasgow. The event will also recognize his contributions to boxing in the Pictou County area, where he is a member of the Pictou County Boxing Hall of Fame. Paris is also in the Canadian Boxing Hall of Fame and the Nova Scotia Sports Heritage Hall of Fame.

When Paris was young, a promoter could put on an entire fight card with boxers from New Glasgow — and half of them could be Parises. Sparky's brother, Percy, held the Maritime and Canadian lightweight championships. His nephew, Keith Paris, was also a crowd-pleasing professional who held the Maritime lightweight title.

Sparky Paris did not have an extensive boxing career. He had about 25 fights, tangling with the likes of Bann Boudreaux, Bob Sevaco, Grant West, Freddie Stewart, Digger MacEwan, Donald Chisholm, Sheldon Campbell, Bob Leahy, and Doug Odo.

Paris remembers how he was first induced to step into the ring: "When I was 18 years old, two men approached me and asked if I wanted to fight at the St. John's Bowl in New Glasgow. I said 'Sure.' They put me in with Dave Melanson, and I beat him in five rounds. We fought again later, and it came out a draw."

Paris credits his trainers — Jerry Bowden, Russell and Bob Paris and Babe Whalen — for his success in the ring. And it was as a trainer that Paris made his greatest mark in local boxing history. Not only did he train Keith and Percy Paris; he also taught the sweet science to Joe Borden, Gordy Maclean, Jo Jo Jackson, Barry Pilgrim, Raymond Jackson, and Bearcat Jackson.

Paris ran The Paris Boys Gym in New Glasgow from 1942 to 1964. At one time, he had 40 fighters — amateur and professional, black and white — sparring and hitting the bags in his gym.

He gave up his gym for two reasons: "The boys just weren't as interested in boxing as they used to be," he says. "And it was starting to cost me too much money to run the place, what with insurance and all."

Outside the boxing arena, Paris has owned and operated a trucking business for the past 50 years. He started working as a newspaper carrier at the age of eight. Before he started his trucking business, he hauled gravel and worked at Maritime Steel.

In real life and in fiction, boxing is often portrayed as a brutal sport that chews fighters up and spits them out. Unfortunately, there's some truth in that stereotype. But there are many exceptions that defy that rule. Paris is one of them.

"I made a little money when I was fighting," he recalls. "But I was in it for the love of the game. Today, it's all about money. The fighters act like they don't love the sport anymore."

Still, Paris wouldn't discourage a young athlete from getting into boxing today. "If he was interested, I'd say go ahead."

Paris and his wife, Ruth, have three daughters: Marie Symonds of Dartmouth and Aretha and Sherri Borden of Halifax, all of whom are doing well. They look forward to seeing family and friends gather in tribute to a man who "coulda been a contender" in the ring, and has been a champion in life.

Black journalists form new group
February 1, 1998

Last month, the Black Journalists Association of Nova Scotia (BJANS) held its official launch at the Black Cultural Centre for Nova Scotia. Although the event happened to fall on the coldest Thursday night yet this winter, the turnout was impressive. It was as though word had circulated in the community that the evening would be an historic occasion, something that shouldn't be missed. And so it was.

Sheryl Grant, who is lifestyle editor for *The Chronicle-Herald—Mail-Star*, delivered the keynote speech. Grant has been at *The Herald* for 17 years, and she spoke of her experiences as the only black person in that paper's newsroom during her first 10 years there. She also emphasized the need for more local hiring of black students who are attending King's College School of Journalism and other media-training institutions.

Other speakers included Environment Minister Wayne Adams, Halifax West MP Gordon Earle, and Preston Councillor David Hendsbee, as well as representatives from King's and other educational outlets.

The speeches were punctuated with African drumming by Wayn Hamilton and Henry Bishop. As well, the singing of the Colley Family — Joe and Lela and their son, Shaune — made the audience forget how cold it was outside.

Another highlight of the evening was the debut of *Breaking Through*, a documentary video produced by BJANS about the experiences of black workers in Nova Scotia's media outlets. After the speeches ended, BJANS members, people from the media, and people from the community mingled.

Aside from one sour note, it was a positive experience for all involved. The sour note was sounded by Alex J. Walling of the Atlantic Broadcasting and Media Institute.

During his speech Walling, by accident or design, gave the impression he thinks the reason there aren't more blacks in the media is that we all want to start at the top and don't want to take entry-level jobs and work our way up like everybody else.

That impression is dead wrong. What blacks want is the same access "everybody else" has to entry-level positions — no more, and damn well no less.

Aside from the Walling episode, the launch of BJANS was historic because it demonstrated the inroads blacks have made into the mainstream media in this province. It also showed the distance that has to be travelled before black journalists become part of the mainstream instead of anomalies swimming in isolation.

Thanks to the can-do spirit behind the formation of BJANS, that distance has become narrower.

The seed that grew into BJANS was planted last year, when Sherri Borden, a staff reporter for *The Chronicle-Herald—Mail-Star* and eventual president of BJANS, attended a convention of the National Association of Black Journalists in Chicago.

Her experiences there inspired her to start a similar organization here. Last September, local black media workers and students gathered at King's College for a meet-and-greet session.

From that starting point, momentum gathered. The group soon established its objectives, which include assisting journalists in furthering and enhancing their careers; recognizing the professional advancement of blacks in the news media; improving communications between blacks and the mainstream media; and improving media coverage of blacks across Nova Scotia.

Eventually, BJANS hopes to establish scholarship funds to help black students to obtain the training needed for careers in the news media.

The success of the launch was a major step toward the fulfillment of those objectives. It showcased the wide scope of black participation in media outlets.

Black reporters can be seen on local television broadcasts and heard on the radio. Halifax's two daily newspapers boast black columnists, reporters and editors.

And, behind the scenes, black technicians do the work that brings news broadcasts onto screens and airwaves.

Today's black media workers are not the first in the field. In his speech at the BJANS launch, Adams acknowledged such journalistic pioneers as Aleta Williams, who has been in the business more than 40 years; Dr. Carrie Best, who began a black newspaper in the 1940s; and George Borden, who wrote for several black newspapers and has hosted mainstream TV shows. Adams himself was once a broadcast journalist.

Those and other trailblazers opened the doors for blacks in the media. Today's black media workers walked through those doors and continued the tradition those forerunners established. And it is now our responsibility to keep those doors open so that the next generation can enter.

By that time, there should be so many proven black workers in the field that the doors to Nova Scotia media outlets will never be closed again.

Gordon Earle's year of making history in Ottawa
May 31, 1998

Last year, Gordon Earle made history by becoming Nova Scotia's first black Member of Parliament. Earle, who won Halifax West for the NDP in a federal election that saw six NDP MPs elected, along with five Progressive Conservatives and no Liberals, recently reflected on his first year in office.

"It has certainly lived up to my expectations," he says. "Very busy, very challenging, and offers lots of opportunities to serve my constituents and society in general."

His most memorable Parliamentary moment so far?

"Probably my first speech, responding to the throne speech when the 36th Parliament opened in September '97," Earle says. "Also, my recent speech on the question of compensation for all victims who contracted hepatitis C through tainted blood.

"Both those occasions provided an opportunity to speak from the heart on matters I deeply believe in — treating people fairly, with love and respect."

In his hepatitis C speech, Earle said: "The money will take care of itself. We have to let the heart rule in this matter."

Those two sentences effectively sum up the argument of those who believe all victims of hepatitis C should receive compensation, not just those who were infected between 1986 and 1990.

However, speeches in the Commons are only a small part of an MP's life. Much of their work involves dealing with constituent and community concerns, such as Canada Pension Plan benefits, immigration and employment problems, and highway-safety issues. Matters specific to the Halifax West riding include the Upper Hammonds Plains Road water project, lighthouse preservation, and requests for new schools.

"I've addressed these matters by establishing an effective constituency office, with caring and dedicated assistants — Gwen Lambert and Shingai Nyajeka — who take up the concerns directly with the government departments involved," says Earle.

NDP Leader Alexa McDonough appointed Earle as the party's critic for Aboriginal Affairs and Northern Development. In that capacity, and as a member of parliamentary committees on aboriginal concerns and economic development, he has addressed issues such as the new Nunavut territory and the Mi'kmaq education bill.

He has also spoken out on aboriginal health concerns, saying: "Health and social conditions in aboriginal communities are disastrous and clearly unacceptable under Canadian standards."

The NDP exceeded expectations in its performance in the last federal election, winning 21 seats to regain its official-party status. Of his party's performance in office, Earle says: "I would give both our party and our leader top marks. I feel that our leader has been very focused, knowledgeable, dedicated and hard-working, giving us high profile both in the House of Commons and across the nation. The party has worked well as a team on behalf of those we represent, and the goals and objectives upon which we based our election campaign.

"I believe the other parties, and the government in particular, have heard our voice on behalf of Canadians, and I believe we have made a difference."

Earle is not the only black Member of Parliament. Previously, black MPs were elected one at a time — Lincoln Alexander for the Conservatives during the 1960s and '70s, and Howard McCurdy for the NDP in the 1980s and '90s. Now, along with Earle, there are other black MPs, such as Ovid Jackson and Jean Augustine of Ontario. Also, there are three black senators: Anne Cools of Ontario, and Donald Oliver and Calvin Ruck of Nova Scotia.

In the U.S., blacks in Congress formed their own caucus, which has been effective in advancing black political concerns. But Earle is skeptical about the likelihood of a similar caucus forming in Parliament.

"I don't think the formation of a black caucus, as in the U.S. House, will happen," he says. "I don't think it is necessary in that sense. I think the important thing is having the presence that we have, and while we may from time to time, as black members, support causes of common concern, I don't think we need a formal black caucus to do that. I think the political backgrounds of the various individuals would probably hinder such an enterprise."

Earle's plans for the coming year include learning more about his critic area and the rules of the House of Commons, and getting to know more members of the House on a personal basis. He is also working on a private member's bill, the subject matter of which will be revealed in the future.

"I entered politics not to let politics change me, but rather that I hopefully would be able to bring some change to politics," he says. "I will continue to work, with God's help, to show that we can and indeed we must in the world of politics, and indeed in all professions, treat our fellow human beings fairly, and with love and respect."

So far, he is doing just that, and doing it well.

Cultural Centre celebrates success
October 11, 1998

On October 17, the Black Cultural Society will hold two celebrations in one. This year marks the 15th anniversary of the Black Cultural Centre for Nova Scotia, an institution that is unique in Canada — the first of its kind.

The October 17 event will honor not only the decade-and-a-half the centre has been doing its work; it will also pay tribute to Calvin Ruck, who was recently appointed to the Senate. The theme for the celebration is Night of the Senator.

Although the centre first opened its doors in September of 1983, its genesis goes back to 1972. At that time, Rev. William P. Oliver conceived the idea of a centre that would be not only a repository of the history of blacks in this province, but also a focal point for the continuing development of the community's culture. At the time, that might have seemed little more than a pipe dream, as the resources of the Nova Scotian black population were limited. But the greatest resource of all is determination. Rev. Oliver and those who worked with him, including the provincial Department of Education and the Black United Front, as well as Donald Oliver, Rev. P.A. Best, Geraldine Browning, Hamid Rasheed, Edith Cromwell, Rev. Donald Skeir, Neville Gibson, Ken Pinto, H.A.J. (Gus) Wedderburn, and Joan Browne, possessed that resource in abundance.

Oliver wrote a proposal that articulated the black community's need for a cultural centre. In it, he stated: "One means to remedy and overcome cultural awareness within any minority group is the provision of an adequate facility where they can be exposed to their own culture and at the same time share their culture with other cultural groups. Both functions must be performed concurrently."

And in that principle lies the strength of the centre. Although its purpose is to preserve black history and develop black culture, it does not exclude others from participating in either of those functions. The centre's doors have always been open to everyone.

In 1977, the Society for the Protection and Preservation of Black Culture in Nova Scotia, more commonly known as the Black Cultural Society, was founded. The immediate goal of the society was to raise money for the building of the centre.

Five years passed between the birth of the society and the sod-turning ceremony for the construction of the centre in 1982. Fund-raising efforts netted $1.2 million from sources that included the federal and provincial governments as well as the municipalities of Halifax, Dartmouth, Sydney, Bedford, Liverpool, Shelburne, Springhill, and Yarmouth. The counties of Halifax, Queens, Guysborough, and Lunenburg also participated, as did numerous businesses, groups and individuals.

The centre was built on land bought from an older black Nova Scotian institution, the Nova Scotia Home for Colored Children. Since its founding, it has grown under the stewardship of executive directors Wayne Adams and Dr. Bridglal Pachai, and its curator, Henry Bishop.

Bishop has held the curator's position since the centre first opened, and before that, he was involved in its planning. When asked what he thinks the centre's greatest accomplishment has been, his reply came without hesitation: "Without question, our greatest accomplishment has been our effect on children. Education is the epitome of why we are here. We can celebrate our events, our successes, and our programs. But the children are most important. When they're here, I can see in their eyes the effects of what they are learning about black people. And those are the eyes of the future."

Over the years, the centre has firmly established itself as a provincial community institution, providing displays, a library, archives, audiovisual materials, and an amphitheatre for performances and lectures. The centre also houses an RCMP community-policing office. Bishop estimates that tens of thousands of visitors have passed through its doors, either individually or in tour groups.

The centre also has some ambitious plans for the future.

"We want to expand our facility for theatre and drama," Bishop says. "We also want to develop a science and computer centre, and a recording studio."

The centre's upcoming celebration is well-deserved. The keynote speaker for the event will be actor/producer Anthony Sherwood. Special guests include Lt. Gov. James Kinley, Senators Donald Oliver and Anne Cools, and Liberal MP Jean Augustine.

Africville:
The spirit lives

Of all the black communities in Nova Scotia, the one with which I most identify is one that no longer exists — on the map, anyway. That community is Africville.

Africville was bulldozed during the 1960s in the name of urban renewal and integration. However, even though its houses are long gone, Africville lives on in the hearts and souls of its people, and its story is far from finished.

In 1989, it was my privilege to write part of the catalogue for *Africville: A Spirit That Lives On*, an exhibit organized by the Mount Vincent University Art Gallery, the Africville Genealogy Society, the Black Cultural Centre for Nova Scotia, and the National Film Board, Atlantic Centre.

Even though I'm a come-from-away, I formed a bond with the community and people of Africville. What happened to them could easily have happened to the community in which I was raised.

A grassy space called Seaview Park now occupies the space where Africville once stood. Although many of its former residents and their descendants still live in the Halifax area, many others have dispersed throughout the rest of Canada and the United States — an Africville diaspora.

Wherever they have gone, however, they have taken part of Africville with them. And one day, in the near or distant future, those parts will become whole again.

Former Africville residents gather for reunion in July, 1996.
(Darrell Oake/The Daily News)

Africville — What if?

July 30, 1989

> *"Soon Africville will be but a name. And, in the not too*
> *distant future that, too, mercifully will be forgotten."*
>   – Halifax newspaper editorial, 1967

Things didn't quite work out that way, did they? Twenty-two years after the above comment was written, Africville remains more than just a name. And this weekend's reunion of relocated Africville residents at Seaview Park is ample evidence that the community is far from "forgotten" — mercifully or otherwise.

Seaview Park, with its grassy slopes, paved pathways, and wooden benches, looks like most other low-key recreational facilities. It's a place to walk, to sit quietly, to gaze at the still waters of the Bedford Basin. Once a year, however, the park becomes a different place. Once a year, the Africville Genealogy Society sponsors a gathering of the people whose homes once stood on this scenic site.

The houses they lived in are long gone, chewed to kindling by the steel teeth of bulldozers. But on Reunion Day, you can almost see their outlines take shape as the older residents point out locations to children born long after the relocation. Many of the people who lived in and fought for the community have long since died. Yet you can still hear the whisper of their voices beneath the hum of conversation as long-separated relatives meet and reminisce. And when the Sunday Memorial Service is over, and the park is quiet again, the whispers will remain, as will the unseen silhouettes of the houses and the church for which the park was named.

For Seaview Park is haunted — not by the ghosts of the departed, but by the spectres of misunderstanding, miscalculation, and the kind of "good intentions" that are said to pave the road to Hell.

In the years that have gone by since the relocation, much has been written about the move as a "social experiment" that somehow went amiss. "Urban renewal" and "integration" were the watchwords of social change in the early 1960s. "Progress" was the banner under which the destroyers of a 130-year-old community marched. Those who resisted the inevitable erasure of Africville from the face of Halifax were criticized as opponents of "progress." "Progress" was envisioned in the form of massive industrial development along the Bedford Basin and happy Africville families dispersed in white neighborhoods.

When Africvilleans made it known that they did not want their community broken up, they were accused of being "afraid of integration." And in the early 1960s, that accusation was a heavy cross to bear. At that time, predominantly black communities, churches, and businesses were viewed strictly as examples of segregation. From that viewpoint, the merits and achievements of black institutions didn't matter. Segregation was segregation, and it had to go. That bedrock philosophical stance was the foundation of the civil-rights movement as well as the political thought of black and white liberals of the time.

What if the people of Africville had been better organized when Halifax City Council made the final relocation decision in 1962? What if stronger internal leadership had emerged, and more effective tactics for resistance developed? Would Africville still be standing today?

Questions such as these have eaten at former Africville residents for two decades. In retrospect, the answer is, "Probably not."

A black community that was perceived as fighting to stay "segregated" would not have gained much sympathy in the early 1960s. The strongest organization Africville could have mustered would most likely have had to fight its battle without allies. Integration was the Holy Grail then. Anyone seen as turning away from it was considered worse than a fool. Resistance to the relocation was also resistance to social forces that were sweeping North America.

Africville would not have had enough fingers to place in the leaking dike. The community was fated to serve as an example, both to its own residents and those of other black settlements in Nova Scotia.

When the last house in Africville fell in 1970, the relocation issue was thought to have been buried beneath the rubble. And if Africville had truly been nothing more than a collection of houses that lacked sewerage and running water, the prediction in that 1967 headline would have come true.

But Africville was more than that. It was tradition; it was family; it was, above all else, home. The annual reunion is but one of many signs that the community remains alive and well. Twenty years after the houses went down, the story of Africville is far from finished.

And the whispers in Seaview Park continue to ride the breeze from the Basin.

The Africville exhibit carried the story of the community across Canada, and opened more than a few eyes.

Spirit:
A little bit of "home" in Toronto
September 2, 1990

In 1966, Toronto's *Star Weekly* magazine ran a feature story titled "The Slow and Welcome Death of Africville." At that time, conventional wisdom held that the bulldozing of the 130-year-old black community on the shores of the Bedford Basin was a good thing. Variously described as a "slum," a "ghetto," and an "eyesore," Africville was viewed as an example of the kind of racial segregation thought to exist only in Mississippi, Alabama, or South Africa.

To well-meaning bureaucrats and social planners of the 1960s, the erasure of Africville from the map and the relocation of its residents constituted an affirmation of Canada as a "just society." It was supposed to confirm that this country was nothing like an American South wracked by beatings and bombings related to the civil rights movement.

If the Africville residents didn't agree with that line of reasoning — too bad. One day, they'd come to realize that the relocation was done "for their own good". . .

Two and a half decades later, Toronto's headlines about Africville have changed:

Visit Africville And See Inside Our Own Bigotry — *The Toronto Star*, July 31, 1990
The Fight To Regain A Lost Home — *The Globe and Mail*, August 20, 1990

Those headlines refer to the Toronto tenure of *Africville: A Spirit That Lives On*, a multi-media exhibit that had its debut at the Mount Saint Vincent University Art Gallery back in October of 1989. In Toron-

189

to, the exhibit was displayed from July 28 to August 19 at the York Quay Gallery at the Harbourfront complex. Over the next two years, *Spirit* will travel to Vancouver, Charlottetown, Winnipeg, Montreal, and the Museum of Civilization in Ottawa. After its travelling itinerary is done, the exhibit will be on permanent display at the Black Cultural Center for Nova Scotia.

By all standards, *Spirit's* three-week Harbourfront run was an unqualified success. After an opening that featured a moving address by Ontario Lieutenant-Governor Lincoln Alexander, an estimated 6,500 visitors strolled through designer Stephen Osler's symbolic reconstruction of Africville. Some of the comments visitors scribbled in the guest book are revealing:

> "Never give up the fight . . ."
> "The government should be in shame . . ."
> "The black people, like the Indians, deserve support
> – moral and financial . . ."

Twenty-five years ago, comments like these would have been inconceivable outside the Africville community itself. What has happened over the intervening years to change that? Perhaps an experience thought to be unique and isolated then can be perceived as universal today.

An interesting sidelight to *Spirit's* Toronto opening was the lingering controversy over an earlier exhibit: the Royal Ontario Museum's *Into The Heart of Africa*. The subject of *Heart* was 19th- and early 20th-century Africa as seen through the eyes of British and Canadian missionaries. That viewpoint prompted accusations of "racism" and "stereotyping" from some elements in Toronto's black community. The exhibit even became a target for picketers.

No such protests greeted *Spirit*. Blacks and whites alike perused the artifacts and photographs on display. Carrie Toussaint, an Africville descendant who worked as co-registrar for the exhibit, said most visitors were "fascinated" and "impressed" by their encounter with a long-lost slice of history.

Toronto Star columnist Michele Landsberg made a pointed reference to the inclusion of the Africville Genealogical Society along with Mount Saint Vincent University, the Black Cultural Centre, and the National Film Board in the planning and development of the exhibit. "Take a lesson, ROM," Landsberg chided in her review of *Spirit*.

But the ROM is not the only representative of the establishment that needs to "take a lesson" from the success of *Spirit*. Municipal and provincial governments across Canada could learn valuable lessons from the Africville experience. The survival of pride, kinship, and a sense of belonging among the residents of Africville and their descendants is proof positive that a community doesn't have to die — "slowly" or otherwise — even when its land is expropriated, its buildings torn down, and its people scattered to the winds.

How has the exhibit affected Africville? One answer may be found in the reflections of Joanne Toussaint, who was born after the relocation. "I'm glad our story is being carried across the country," she says. "But the exhibit is like a piece of 'home'. I'll be happy when 'home' returns to Halifax."

Africville residents did more than bask in the glory of the exhibit. By the end of 1990, they began to take action to reclaim their lost legacy. That action began with opposition to a proposed industrial road.

The dream of a new Africville
December 3, 1990

Once again, the dislocated black community of Africville is in the news.

The Africville story is well-known. For more than a century, the community clung to existence on the shores of the Bedford Basin, geographically part of Halifax but socially in another world. Despite the city's continual refusal to provide such basic services as sewerage and water lines, Africville remained a vital, unique component of Nova Scotian culture until it was bulldozed out of existence in the mid-1960s. Although the land was slated for eventual "industrial development," it remained idle until 1985, when Seaview Park was established there.

Some former Africville residents and their descendants accepted the inevitable and retained only bittersweet memories of their vanished home. Others cherished a dream of a future return to the land previous generations had owned.

Now the dreamers have begun to act. Recently, the Africville Genealogy Society announced plans to launch legal action against the City of

Halifax. The purpose of such action would be to retrieve the land expropriated back in the 1960s. If the land is returned, housing would be re-established there.

Halifax Mayor Ron Wallace was quick to react, declaring: "If Africville remained today, the city would be severely reprimanded for promoting segregation."

Irvine Carvery, President of the Africville Genealogy Society, disagrees. In Carvery's view, Wallace's segregation argument is a red herring, a distraction. "Is the mayor saying that other historically black communities like Beechville and the Prestons 'promote segregation'?" Carvery wonders.

Indeed, the segregation issue was one of the factors that led to the demolition of the community and the dispersal of its residents. The conventional wisdom of the early 1960s was that all-black communities were by definition segregated and therefore undesirable. What the residents of such communities thought about their situation was considered irrelevant, the reasoning being that they were too ignorant to know what was good for them.

Mayor Wallace's comments betray an unfortunate tinge of this kind of condescension. He implies that the Society is seeking a return to the days of overt racial separation, the days when whites and blacks were confined to their own parts of town by custom, if not by law.

The segregation argument dredges up stereotypes of Africville that are a quarter of a century old and only partially offset by the more positive images of the multi-media exhibit that is now travelling across the country. The garbage dump, the lack of sewerage and running water, the muddy, unpaved roads . . . those were the images that made it easy for the city to push its relocation plan. The segregation issue was the gasoline that filled the tanks of the bulldozers as they destroyed Africville's houses. Is that what you want to return to? the opponents of a re-establishment of Africville ask incredulously.

The answer is "No." The Africville Genealogy Society is not advocating any such backward step. A new Africville would not be an all-black community, and it would have all the amenities that were deliberately withheld in the past.

"We're not saying all the former Africville residents and their descendants would want to return to the site," says Carvery. "If housing is re-established there, we want to have the first priority in obtaining it.

That's only fair, given the circumstances of the relocation. But there'd still be plenty of room for anyone else who wanted to live there."

One of the factors precipitating the Society's decision was CN Rail's proposal to build a container terminal that would include an access road through Seaview Park. A road like that, with constant heavy-vehicle traffic, would be a hindrance to any kind of residential development.

Ironically, it was railroads that began the downfall of the community. Through the last half of its life, Africville was sliced by three rail lines that were built on expropriated land. Industrial roads would have the same disruptive effect.

Although the Society is determined to press its claim, it must overcome a formidable obstacle. As anyone involved in aboriginal land claims can attest, it takes money to mount a challenge in the court system. Strictly speaking, the Africville situation is not the same as that of Native Canadians, whose claim to their lands goes back thousands of years. Still, the bureaucratic barriers both groups face are remarkably similar.

The Africville Genealogy Society is long on determination, but short of cash. Fundraising efforts have begun. Hopefully, the people of Africville will eventually win the justice that eluded them during the 1960s.

Battle lines are drawn
May 19, 1991

Although its stint in the headlines passed about a month ago, the Seaview Park access road issue is still destined to become a major point of confrontation involving city politics, the environment, and race relations.

At first glance, the situation appears straightforward. The Halifax Port Corporation wants to use federal funds to build a road through Seaview Park, the site of Africville, for the purpose of linking Fairview Cove to Richmond Terminal.

Former residents of Africville, as well as their descendants and sympathizers, do not want the road to pass through the park. To them, the park is all that remains of their former home, a place where old memories can be revived and shared with others.

Those memories have a deep resonance, which was evident at a recent anti-road meeting, where a call for non-violent civil disobedience to block construction of the road received enthusiastic support.

Those who attended the meeting cited two reasons for considering such drastic tactics. First, they believe the presence of an industrial road will compromise the quality of Seaview Park because of the noise and pollution caused by a steady stream of 18-wheel trucks. Second, they resent Halifax City Council's refusal to hold public hearings on the matter before bringing it to a vote.

Soon after the meeting, Halifax Mayor Ron Wallace wrote a rebuttal that was published on *The Mail-Star's* opinion page. Responding to criticism by the Black United Front and the Africville Genealogy Society, Wallace raised several points.

First, he indicated that the road would not "encroach even one inch" on Seaview Park lands. To him, it would only be an upgrading of the extension of Barrington Street that was once the main road through Africville.

Wallace's second point was that the public (including the road's critics) had six different opportunities to address City Council on the issue, but no one ever took advantage of those opportunities.

Finally, Wallace indicated that the road would aid in the improvement of port facilities. "This project is vital in assisting the port to remain competitive," he wrote. "If necessary port improvements are delayed, the risk of losing business at the port becomes even greater."

Does the economic future of the Port of Halifax really hinge on the construction of a single access road in a single, specific location?

Not according to Victor Bayne, executive director of the Halifax-Dartmouth Port Development Commission. Commenting on the economic problems of the port, Bayne cited high Canadian rail costs and depressed ocean rates as contributing factors. The current lack of an access road between Fairview Cove and Richmond Terminals was not mentioned.

As for the Mayor's other contentions, there is more than meets the eye. The road may not "encroach" directly on the land designated as Seaview Park. But it does alter the atmosphere of the terrain, in more ways than one.

Seaview Park does not encompass all the land that was once Africville. The sites of the old Seaview Church and the former Africville Elementary School lie outside the park's boundary. And, according to Africville Genealogy Society President Irvine Carvery, the current route of the access road will pass directly over those two significant sites.

"Encroaching an inch" on Seaview Park is one matter. Obliterating the two locations that mean the most to former Africville residents is something else again.

Concerning the road's status as an extension of Barrington Street, Carvery's memory of the old Africville Road's location in relation to the proposed access road tells him that the two routes are not one and the same. The original road ran through what is now Seaview Park; the proposed road skirts park territory.

As for Wallace's criticism of road opponents' failure to address City Council meetings — presentations from individuals who may or may not manage to make it onto the agenda are never as effective as a public hearing, where many viewpoints are expressed. Also, it is interesting to note that public hearings and ecological studies will be an integral part of the process leading to the development of the proposed Mainland Commons recreational area in Fairview. Why should Seaview Park rate less consideration than the Mainland Commons?

And so the battle lines are drawn. City Council is determined to go ahead with the road; Irvine Carvery is willing to go to jail to stop it. But the underlying issues are much more complicated than they appear to be.

Park may become an eyesore
May 20, 1991

At first glance, the current dispute over the fate of Seaview Park could be viewed as a confrontation between development and sentiment; the future and the past; or even black and white. But the issues aren't that simple. They never have been.

In his *Daily News* column, Tom Regan wrote that the plan to run an industrial road through the park was viewed as a "business decision" by Halifax City Council (or, at least, the Council members who voted in its favor) and the Halifax Port Corporation. That assessment is correct, up to a point. It can, however, be taken a step farther. This wasn't just a business decision. It was also a power decision.

What kind of power? Coercive power . . . the kind that says: "We're going to go ahead and do this, and it doesn't much matter what anybody else thinks." This is the same kind of power Council exerted almost 30 years ago, when the wheels of the Africville relocation were cranked into motion.

The current decision has failed to take into account the heritage value of the Seaview Park site, which was once an established black community. It was a decision that ignored the significance the Africville experience holds for its former residents, their descendants, the rest of the black community, and the province as a whole.

The timing of the road project is interesting. And a look back to recent history is instructive. A road in the Seaview Park area was first proposed in 1984, a year before the park officially opened. At that time, the purpose of the road was to link Fairview Cove to the Volvo assembly plant. Then the Volvo plant relocated, and that was the end of plans for the road. The city established Seaview Park in 1985. Was it known then that the park would enjoy only six years of undisturbed existence?

Fast-forward to 1989. During the latter part of that year, the *Africville: A Spirit That Lives On* exhibit opened at the Mount St. Vincent University Art Gallery. The exhibit, which featured displays of artifacts salvaged from the Africville relocation, put the community back on the map of social consciousness.

During the weekend of the opening, a conference concerning the past, present, and future of Africville produced a wide-ranging series of discussions. Out of those discussions came a firm resolve to right the old wrong, to reclaim the lost land. A year later, the Africville Genealogy Society announced its intention to pursue legal action toward that end.

A few months after that, the access road that died in 1984 lurched back to life. Suddenly, the road became essential to the economic survival of the port.

The timing of City Council's decision to go ahead with the road could, of course, be coincidental. On the other hand, it could also represent a pre-emptive strike designed to stymie the Africville residents' efforts to recover what once belonged to them.

A public hearing or inquiry would help to clarify these matters. It would also shed light on why alternate access routes, such as the one Africville Genealogy Society President Irvine Carvery proposed in the April 21 *Daily News*, were not considered, and why there wasn't an environmental-impact study of the effects of a truck road on the park.

When the original Africville relocation scheme unfolded in the 1960s, the media portrayed the community as an "eyesore." And that was one of the milder epithets employed.

Ostensibly, the people in power did not want motorists crossing the proposed MacKay Bridge to pass directly over a black community that had become an outpost of urban poverty and neglect. Of course, the city's prominent role in the creation of those conditions was conveniently ignored.

In the near future, commuters travelling over the MacKay Bridge may be greeted by the sight of bulldozers once again chewing up what used to be Africville. They may also see peaceful protesters attempting to block the progress of those bulldozers. They may see police dragging those protesters away, while more line up to take their places.

And that will be an eyesore of a different kind — a moral eyesore.

Park intervention is progress
June 17, 1991

The provincial government's recent intervention into the Seaview Park road controversy is welcome news. It indicates that someone, somewhere, is at least listening to objections against the road raised by the Africville Genealogy Society and its supporters.

In summary, the following sequence of events led up to the government's decision:

The Halifax Port Commission and Halifax City Council announced a proposed truck road linking two container piers.

The Africville Genealogy Society objected to the road on the grounds that it would damage the recreational, historical, and ecological integrity of the park, which is also the site of the former Africville community.

Halifax Mayor Ron Wallace wrote an article in *The Mail-Star* declaring that the road was essential to the survival of the port and that it will "not encroach one inch" on Seaview Park land.

The AGS and other interested parties promised further protest, including possible civil disobedience, if the road went through as planned.

The provincial government intervened.

In the past, the last part of the scenario would never have happened. The road would have gone through, no matter what. Objections would have been dismissed or explained away. The real significance of the site to its former residents would have been dismissed as irrelevant. And intimations of protests and civil disobedience would have been ignored, just as they were when Africville was bulldozed during the 1960s.

Thus, the government's decision to intervene represents progress.

The study, which is expected to take six weeks to complete, will be conducted by two government departments along with the port corporation. All this for the amazingly modest cost of $15,000 — a price even the frugality-minded Tory provincial government could not refuse.

Regardless of any possible political ramifications, the implementation of the engineering study is encouraging. Still, any celebration of the government's decision may be premature.

In itself the study is not a solution to the problem. It's only a study. No one can predict its results, or the reception it will receive when it is presented to City Council.

What if the engineers confirm City Council's decision to run the road through (or past — the distinction still isn't clear) the park? What if they recommend an alternative route that is not acceptable to Council and the port corporation?

At best, the study could signal the beginning of an acceptable settlement of the impasse between Council and the Africville Genealogy Society. That, however, is just a hope. The study might also represent one more step along a road that will ultimately lead to confrontation. Still, the government's intervention is in itself a milestone.

But hold the champagne, folks. This story has yet to run its course.

Park road takes more twists
November 25, 1991

Over the past year or so, the saga of the Seaview Park access road has undergone more twists and turns than a rattlesnake on an LSD trip. Last spring, Halifax City Council approved the construction of a road to provide access for trucks to the Richmond Terminal. Under the original plan, the road would have passed through land originally occupied by Africville.

The Africville Genealogy Society protested the route of the road. Whether or not the road actually encroached on park land wasn't the point. The source of the anger and recrimination was the prospect of a stream of 18-wheelers thundering hourly past a place of historic significance not only to the black community, but also to Canada as a whole.

As a result of intense criticism, the construction of the road was postponed pending a study of alternate routes commissioned by Industry, Trade, and Technology Minister Tom McInnis. Although the final recommendations of that study are still pending, a compromise solution seemed inevitable.

Last week, a tentative agreement was announced. The road would be built farther away from the park than previously planned, and the Seaview Baptist Church, which was the heart of the old Africville community, would be reconstructed.

This was a classic *quid pro quo*. The original route of the road would have passed over the sites of the church and the school. Those sites were not part of Seaview Park land. In exchange for putting up with a road closer to the park than they would have wanted, the Africville descendants would regain an important part of their heritage.

Of course, both aspects of this outcome were subject to negotiation. Canadian National owns some of the land necessary for the new route. Supposedly, negotiations for its acquisition were already underway. That's when the latest twist in the road occurred.

"Negotiations? What negotiations? Nobody told us about any negotiations," said a CN spokesman the day after the compromise was announced. Now it appears that the true ownership of the land in question is a mystery.

How many more bends and curves will this road follow before it finally runs into a dead end?

The so-called "vital" port road has yet to be built.

Africville:
The spirit is stronger than ever
August 2, 1992

For the past nine years, the last weekend in July has marked a time of reunion and remembrance for the people who once lived in Africville. Since 1985, the reunions have occurred in Seaview Park, a recreational area that covers the ground upon which a black community endured for more than 100 years.

The event, which attracts former Africville residents, descendants, and friends from the breadth of Canada and the United States, has always been a time of reflection on the past and renewal of hope for the future. Sadness was there as well. Many former Africville residents continued to mourn the bulldozing of their community in the 1960s.

In most of the recent reunions, the weather reflected that mood. Rain would drizzle, shower, or pour from the sky as the people of Africville contemplated the circumstances that led to their relocation nearly 30 years ago.

Last year, the mood of the reunion was dampened not only by rainy weather, but also by the probability that an access road connecting two container piers would damage the integrity of Seaview Park as well as the memory of Africville. Last year's reunion was thus viewed as possibly the last before another violation occurred to the space Africville's spirit occupied.

Before 1991 ended, however, the Africville Genealogy Society and city and port of Halifax officials reached a compromise agreement. The access road would be re-routed farther away from the park. And the provincial government, which had intervened in the dispute, pledged to finance the construction of a replica of Africville's Seaview Baptist Church.

That decision had enormous significance. Of all the memories of the relocation, the dark-of-the-night destruction of the church that was the heart of the community remains the most bitter of all. Its rebirth symbolized the turning of a corner for the people of Africville.

That turn was evident in this year's reunion. It wasn't just the fine weather and high turnout. It was a sense of invitation, an open embrace extended from Africville to the larger Nova Scotia community.

Despite a reputation for clannishness, Africville has never been a closed society. During its pre-relocation existence, the community opened its doors to newcomers from other parts of the province, as well as places as far and wide apart as Barbados and Norway. And people from outside Africville have always been welcome to attend the reunions and share food, drink and memories.

Before this year, though, there was always an impression that the reunions were in part a time of grieving over a loss only former Africville residents could fully feel. Those of us on the outside could understand at a certain level, but we couldn't experience the same kind of emotion as a person who has watched as his or her belongings were carted away in a municipal garbage truck. You just couldn't help feeling as though you were intruding on something private, even though the Africville people never gave that impression.

The feeling was different this year. The grief is still there; it always will be. But there was so much more as well. The whole experience was what a visit to Africville must have been like in the old days, when folks from far and wide came down to be part of the sunrise service at Easter.

This year, the AGS opened the reunion to participation by the International Gospel Festival, Artczar Gallery, and Formac Publishing, which used the occasion to launch its new book, *The Spirit of Africville*. White faces and colorful African garb dotted a crowd estimated at 1,000. Nearly all the faces you saw — black, white and in-between — sported broad smiles.

Martin Luther King III, son of the slain American civil rights leader, did a walkabout in the park on Saturday and helped to break the ground at the site of the new Seaview Church on Sunday. Anybody who might have predicted such an event this time last year wouldn't have been given even the benefit of the doubt. Now the church is expected to be completed in time for next year's reunion, which will probably break all attendance records.

Africville's spirit, which was never extinguished even in the worst of times, is now stronger than ever. Its light shines on everyone, regardless of color.

Africville:
Bulldoze the epitaphs
July 18, 1993

A week from today, the Africville Genealogy Society will open an eight-day celebration of the continuation of a community for which premature epitaphs were written nearly 30 years ago.

During the 1960s Africville, a black community that had struggled on the shore of the Bedford Basin for more than 100 years, was bulldozed in the name of integration and urban renewal. Although most of the community's residents remained in the metro area after they were "relocated," others migrated to other parts of Canada and the United States — an Africville diaspora.

In 1981 three young Africville residents, Linda Mantley, Brenda Steed Ross, and the late Deborah Dixon Jones, founded the Africville Genealogy Society to nurture the spirit of the community and pass its legacy on to future generations. Two years later, the first Africville reunion was held at the site in the shadow of the MacKay Bridge. Seaview Park was officially opened during the 1985 reunion.

The Africville reunion continued, attracting more residents, family and friends as the years went by. This year marks a milestone — the 10th reunion. Rod Dixon, chairman of the Africville Reunion Committee, says he expects a high turnout for the reunion.

"There's been lots of response," he says. "People have been calling from Montreal, Toronto, and the States. Tour groups have asked about making it one of their stops. The event has really taken off. It's bigger than we ever thought it could be."

Even the postponement of what was to be a major event at the reunion hasn't dampened any enthusiasm. Two years ago, the provincial government promised to erect a replica of Africville's Seaview Baptist Church at its original location as part of a compromise that settled a dispute over a service road that was to be located in Seaview Park. The replica would be available for religious services, and it would also house the *Africville: A Spirit That Lives On* exhibit that opened at the Mount St. Vincent University Art Gallery in 1989 and has been touring Canada ever since.

The new church was scheduled to open during this year's reunion. However, construction hasn't started because problems with the City of Halifax regarding the installation of water and sewer facilities — an echo of the problems that led to Africville's destruction in the 1960s.

"It's a disappointment," says Dixon. "The church is on hold. It's caught up in a change in city officials. But one day that church will be there."

The church may be built in time for next year's reunion, or the one after that. This year, however, there is still plenty to enjoy during the week's festivities.

Although this is an Africville reunion, it isn't being held exclusively for former Africville residents and their families. Everyone is welcome at all the activities.

"When we lived in Africville, we took care of each other and helped each other when we needed it," Dixon says. "But we cared about other people too. And that's still the way it is with us. That's why we're still here."

Still here, still going strong. That's the spirit Africville will share with the rest of us next week.

Africville reunion: Nobody's an outsider
July 24, 1994

Ever go to a reunion of a family of which you are not a member? It can get pretty uncomfortable. Sometimes you feel like an outsider, even an interloper, as family members laugh at in-jokes you don't get and keep introducing you to people you know you'll never see again.

Not all family reunions are like that, though. The annual Africville reunion certainly isn't. Everyone is welcome to attend it, and no one is an outsider. It doesn't matter what color you are or where you come from; the experience is open to all.

This weekend will mark the eleventh time the people of Africville have gathered to remember their community, which once stood in the space now occupied by the grassy slopes of Seaview Park. The houses, stores and post office vanished nearly 30 years ago, sacrifices on the altar of urban renewal. Indeed, during the 1960s the very name of Africville became a symbol of the shame of segregation.

But the families who once lived in those houses and patronized the stores and post office refused to allow their community to die. Why should they? Their ancestors had struggled against incredible odds to secure and maintain a foothold on the Bedford Basin for more than a century. The hard work, sacrifice and faith of those ancestors deserves to be remembered by everyone. The community spirit those ancestors instilled in their descendants will long outlive outmoded stereotypes and failed social policies.

You don't hear this kind of talk at the reunion, though. The reunion's purpose is far from political. Africville people save their politics for issues like the safety fence recently erected at the shore of Seaview Park, or the service road that would have cut through the park's grounds, or the delayed construction of a replica of Africville's Seaview United Baptist Church. The original church building was torn down during the relocation, and the replica was promised in 1991.

No, the reunion is a time to renew old friendships and make new ones. It's a time to set up a tent or camper on the spot where your ancestral home once stood. It's a time to catch up on news of those who were born during the past year, and who passed away. It's a time to listen to the older people's stories and enjoy the laughter of children playing in the grass.

It's a time to look at the stone sundial monument in the middle of the park and trace your finger across the engraved names of Africville's founding families. It's a time to gaze out at the waters of the Bedford Basin and marvel that this was the view Africville residents used to see every day. It's a time to wonder about what might have happened if the City of Halifax had chosen to improve Africville rather than tear it down.

But that's all water under the bridge — the MacKay Bridge, which looms high above Seaview Park and provided the pretext for bulldozing Africville.

Wondering what might have been and remembering what was ... that's the soil from which creativity springs. The Africville experience has been a source of inspiration for artists with roots inside and outside the community.

The latest is jazz pianist and composer Joe Sealy, who performed the premiere of his Africville Suite at the Rebecca Cohn Auditorium last Friday.

Although Sealy was born in Montreal, his parents, Joseph Sealy and Loretta Brown, were both natives of Africville. Having spent some time there himself, Sealy was inspired to tell Africville's story in music after his father's death two years ago. The Africville Genealogy Society and JazzEast commissioned the Africville Suite, which will be part of Sealy's new album, *Dual Vision*.

Other Africville-inspired works include: *Africville*, an album by Nova Scotian singer/songwriter Faith Nolan; Remember Africville, a National Film Board video produced by Shelagh Mackenzie; and *The Spirit of Africville*, a book published by Formac. Africville has also figured in the poetry of George Elliott Clarke, Maxine Tynes, and Fred Ward.

Africville is not a memory frozen in the amber of history. It's continuing to grow, to evolve, just as it did from the 1840s to the 1960s. Once it was a place. Now it's a spirit, an icon, a metaphor, a home.

And this weekend, it's a reunion.

During the controversy over the proposed East Lake landfill, Africville's name was invoked as an example of what can happen to black communities that become sites for garbage dumps. When residents of Sackville, a predominantly white community that unwillingly received a landfill in the 1970s, were granted compensation for having had the facility in their backyard, Africville residents said they deserved compensation as well. Africville's claim ignited a heated debate that revealed unresolved racial issues .

Some Hotliners irrational
August 4, 1994

Yesterday's *Daily News* Hotline response to the question of whether or not the City of Halifax should pay compensation to former residents of Africville for the landfill once located there was disappointing — but hardly surprising.

In most Hotline questions involving racial matters, the response has been negative, with most callers supporting the anti-black side of issues ranging from the recommendations of a race-relations committee report tabled a few years ago to the arrest record of an anti-pimping task force.

This time, out of 74 callers, 57 were against compensation for former Africville residents. The issue arose because of the granting of millions of dollars in compensation to the residents of Sackville, which has endured a landfill since 1977 and will continue to do so for the next two and a half years, thanks to Metro Authority's inability to implement a new waste-management plan. When Sackville's compensation plan was announced, some former Africville residents rightly asked: "What about us? If Sackville can get compensation for a dump they didn't want, why shouldn't we?"

The Hotline callers offered plenty of reasons for rejecting compensation to Africville.

Some of those reasons were rational, as in "too much time had gone by and too much had already been done for the former residents to open up the purse again."

There were callers who felt that because Africville was not the only community that had to endure the presence of a landfill, it should not receive any special attention.

But Africville did receive "special attention." It was demolished in the 1960s, and part of the reason for that demolition was the presence of the landfill. There hasn't been any suggestion that Sackville should be razed because of the dump that has outworn its welcome in that location.

Other callers said Seaview Park, which occupies the old site of Africville, and the recently confirmed construction of a replica of the Seaview African United Baptist Church, which was the heart of the old community, is compensation enough.

Seaview Park is used by Africville residents and their descendants as a site for their annual reunion. But that hardly qualifies the facility as compensation. Seaview Park is a City of Halifax facility, and whatever benefits it accrues go to Halifax, not Africville. As for the church replica, it will be a cultural and historical monument, and as such should not be included in any debates about compensation.

Other callers' comments on the issue were irrational — and racist. One person said Africville residents "chose to live where ... the garbage was best." He also said he was "sick of being asked to pay for the sins of his fathers."

Well, some of us are sick of people who repeat the sins of their fathers. And to say that Africville residents chose to live near the dump is to reveal one's ignorance. The Africville community had existed for a century before the city decided to place its landfill there.

Other callers denounced any comparison of the Africville and Sackville situations, saying that the people of Sackville own their homes, unlike the so-called "squatters" of Africville.

This is another case of ignorance. Some residents of Africville may not have possessed title deeds to the land they lived on, but that doesn't automatically make them "squatters." But most of the people there owned their land and houses, as do the residents of Sackville.

And then there was the persistent caller who said he always felt he was stalked by "savages" whenever he went to Africville.

The statement implies the caller visited Africville on more than one occasion. Which begs a question: If the caller disliked Africville so much, why did he continue to go there?

Finally, the 17 Hotline callers who came out in favor of compensation should be saluted for their insight and understanding.

After the 1994 reunion, Africville's protests intensified. Two brothers, Eddie and Victor Carvery, set up a protest camp in Seaview Park. And other members of the community made their feelings clear at a public meeting.

Africville story deserves honorable ending
September 11, 1994

First, emotion. Then facts. That's how residents of Africville, the Halifax black community that was bulldozed during the 1960s, have presented their case for long overdue compensation from the city.

Events over the past few weeks have brought Africville to the forefront of city council's agenda. Not since the '60s has the community been in the headlines so often.

At that time, media coverage was negative, paving the road to a forced relocation of people who could trace their Africville ancestry back several generations. Today's headlines may well signal the righting of an old wrong.

Former Africville residents, some of whom were only children during the relocation, are determined to secure an honorable settlement for the loss of their community. Their quest has been a long one, continuing off and on for nearly 30 years.

Now, the pace of events is accelerating. Since the Africville Reunion in July, a variety of activities has been undertaken, ranging from Edward and Victor Carvery's tent sit-in in Seaview Park to a presentation made by Africville residents at Halifax city hall last week.

What was the catalyst for this surge of action?

Was it the long delay in the construction of the Seaview United Baptist Church replica that was promised in 1992 and reaffirmed — but not built — this year?

Was it the generous compensation Sackville residents are receiving for hosting metro's landfill over the past 17 years, while Africville residents received nothing for hosting a dump, a prison, and an infectious-diseases hospital?

Was it the hostility and lingering racism that greeted Africville residents' initial demands for compensation of their own?

Perhaps it's all that and more. At any rate, Africville residents' anger has been festering for a long time, and it flared at a meeting last month at the North Branch Library regarding compensation. Halifax City Manager Barry Coopersmith found himself the target of 30 years' worth of bitterness and frustration as the residents spoke out. The event was cathartic and instructive, indicating the profound effect the past can have on the present.

Even so, had the matter ended there, the meeting would have been just another gripe session, accomplishing little in the long run. But it didn't end there. The outburst of emotion at the North Branch created an atmosphere that led to a respectful hearing of the facts Africville residents presented during a followup meeting at city hall last week.

The claim for compensation is partly based on a 1967 Halifax city council decision that called for any increase in the value of Africville's land to be placed in an education trust fund for the relocated residents. If nothing else, the simple passage of time has increased the value of that land.

The Africville Genealogy Society's compensation committee has obviously done its homework. Now it's time for the city to honor the promise it made 27 years ago.

Perhaps this is the beginning of an honorable end to the Africville story.

In a related matter, some recent remarks from Deputy Mayor Pat Pottie added little to the Africville dialogue. Pottie told *The Daily News*: "Where we're at right now is they say the city did them wrong — the city maintains it didn't do them wrong."

He went on to say: "The City of Halifax stands strong and proud that we're a good corporate community, and I don't think the city would treat their people unfairly. I don't think it's ever happened."

On a scale of sheer ignorance, those comments are on a par with what former cabinet minister David Nantes said after the racial fights at Cole Harbour High School five years ago: "There is no racism in the Nova Scotia education system. It doesn't exist."

If Pottie is "proud" of what the city did to Africville, I'd hate to see what he's ashamed of.

Stung by Africville residents' criticisms, the Halifax municipal government struck back with a report that raised more questions than it answered and exacerbated tensions.

Africville report opens old wounds
November 20, 1994

A report submitted recently by Halifax city social planning director Bob Britton should have been one more step in the negotiating process regarding the payment of further compensation to former Africville residents for the loss of their community during the 1960s. Instead, it has reopened old wounds and rekindled bitter emotions.

Earlier this year, the Africville Genealogy Society tabled a formal request for more money on the grounds that the original compensation payments were inadequate. Britton reported that Halifax paid Africville residents a total of $633,749 to expropriate 149 properties, with 11 families getting more than $15,000. He concluded that "the money paid for the Africville properties was at least very fair and perhaps generous."

If those figures were all the report contained, the ball would now be back in the Africville Genealogy Society's court. It would be up to them to refute or contradict Britton's numbers.

It still is. However, the atmosphere for the negotiations has been poisoned by other aspects of Britton's report that have nothing to do with numbers. Those other aspects are the reason Africville Genealogy Society president Irvine Carvery called the report "insulting," "degrading," and filled with "half-truths" and "lies."

One of the former Africville residents' major complaints is that many of them were forced to go on welfare after they were relocated. Britton's report says the relocation coincided with changes in welfare policy that "increased . . . recipients by virtue of changes in eligibility requirements."

This is an example of what Carvery called a "half-truth." Britton's implication is that even if Africville residents had remained where they were, they would have gone on welfare anyway. That's an unwarranted assumption — and an insult.

Britton also equates the "bulldozer" destruction of Africville to a similar fate met by Greenbank, a white neighborhood that was located near what is now Point Pleasant Park. The fate of Greenbank was indeed unjust, and some of its former residents remain resentful to this day. Still, Greenbank and Africville are separate issues, and using one to belittle the other is degrading to both.

As well, the report contains a sentence guaranteed to light a fuse under most of Africville's people: "It seems that over time, myths grew about Africville as an idyllic community, a self-reliant and mutually supportive community."

Myths?

Do former Africville residents gather for a reunion at Seaview Park every summer to honor myths? Did the Africville: A Spirit That Lives On exhibit glorify myths? Are the books, films, songs and poems Africville has inspired all myths?

Many Africville residents show nostalgia for the community they were forced to leave, but that doesn't mean they are denying the deplorable conditions that existed there. They endured those conditions and made the best of them until the relocation became inevitable. And that's no myth.

The report recommends that Halifax donate land in Seaview Park for the reconstruction of the Seaview Baptist Church and create a scholarship fund "specifically for the descendants of Africville residents." Britton's rationale for the offer is that Halifax needs "to recognize the reality of Africville in its history" and "celebrate the contributions the Africville people made to the City."

The offer is a step in the right direction, primarily because something is better than nothing. However, the motives behind it may not be as altruistic as the words "recognition" and "celebrate" imply.

At the end of the report, Britton says that to do nothing at all about the former Africville residents' concerns would leave Halifax "open to considerable negative publicity."

Negative publicity?

During the time that immediately preceded its destruction, Africville was called a blight, a slum, a ghetto, an eyesore, a disgrace, and a shame. In many people's minds, the community was — and still is — defined by the garbage dump the city placed there. Africville residents can tell Halifax all about "negative publicity."

To his credit, Halifax Mayor Walter Fitzgerald has agreed to continue negotiations with the Africville Genealogy Society. He has also appointed two aldermen, Jerry Blumenthal and Larry Uteck, to join in the talks. If they cannot come to an agreement, a third party may be brought in.

They'd better work fast. In less than two years, metro will be bulldozed into a single municipal unit, and if the matter isn't settled by then, it will be back to square one.

As debate over Africville compensation continued, the camp-in by Eddie and Victor Carvery caused increasing embarrassment to city authorities, who began an effort to remove them.

The law of the land
April 2, 1995

We've all heard that it is wrong to take the law into our own hands. But is it right to apply a law before it is enacted?

Halifax Mayor Walter Fitzgerald seems to think so.

Last month, he made the following comment about former Africville residents Edward and Victor Carvery's eight-month sit-in at Seaview Park to protest what they consider inadequate compensation for their community's removal from their land 30 years ago: "People are in the park illegally and we want them off."

To put it charitably, the mayor was jumping the gun. At a March 22 committee-of-the-whole meeting, Halifax city council had approved an ordinance that would prohibit overnight camping at city parks — including Seaview. However, the law did not go into effect until final council approval on Thursday, March 30.

Fitzgerald made his comment on March 24, days before the ordinance was ratified. Eager as he may be to force the Carverys off the site of their former Africville home, they were still there legally on March 24.

Now that the new law is in effect, the Carverys have not been charged, have not made an appearance in court, and have not been tried or convicted. Whatever happened to that basic principle of North American law, "innocent until proven guilty?" For that matter, why does city council think it's worth a $2,000-per-day fine to get the Carverys out of the park?

The ordinance is the culmination of months of tough talk aimed at appeasing area residents and others who complained about the Carverys' presence in the park. Some of the complaints were racially tinged, implying that the Carverys were receiving special treatment because they are black; that the police would have swiftly evicted them had they been white.

The fact that the Carverys' protest violated no law until now made no impression on the complainers. If such a law doesn't exist, pass one, they exhorted city council.

The ordinance appears to be directed specifically toward the Carvery brothers. Recent history indicates that this type of legislation has a short shelf-life, almost always being declared unconstitutional the first time it faces a court appeal.

Take the Henry Morgenthaler case, for example. For more than 20 years Canadian provinces, including Nova Scotia, have passed legislation aimed at preventing him from operating private abortion clinics. And every time Morgenthaler appealed those laws, the courts — including Nova Scotia's — struck them down.

Take former MLA Billy Joe MacLean for another example. After MacLean was convicted of forgery back in 1988, the provincial legislature passed a law intended to prevent him from running for office again. That law was also struck down on appeal.

The purpose of those examples is not to draw any personal comparisons between the Carvery brothers and Morgenthaler and MacLean. The point is that the Canadian judicial system does not take kindly to the passage of laws motivated by the desire to "get" specific individuals. If the Carverys were to be convicted, there is a good chance they would win an appeal, an outcome that would embarrass Halifax more than their presence in the park ever could.

Fitzgerald has denied that the G-7 economic summit in June has anything at all to do with council's efforts to remove the Carverys from Seaview Park. Well, he can say that if he wants to. But he cannot be very pleased about the prospects of the Africville issue being thrust into the spotlight when the world's news media swarm over a newly spiffed-up Halifax this summer.

Imagine Eddie and Victor Carvery pouring out their grievances on the Oprah Winfrey show.

Imagine Irvine Carvery, president of the Africville Genealogy Society, being interviewed on The Today Show by Bryant Gumbel or Katie Couric.

Imagine Mayor Fitzgerald undergoing a grilling by CNN's Wolf Blitzer.

Imagine the entire history of Africville and its relocation revisited on a segment of 60 Minutes.

The G-7 summit has the potential to put both Halifax and Africville on the map of international media consciousness. But of course that has nothing to do with the passage of a law intended to get the Carverys out of the park. Nothing at all ....

Yeah, right.

Unfortunately, the furore surrounding their protest is threatening to become a wedge that could threaten solidarity among former Africville residents. There are important issues on the bargaining table, including a scholarship fund the city promised to Africville descendants, the building of a replica of the old Seaview Baptist Church, and a revisiting of compensation payments for land lost in the 1960s.

Leaders of the Africville Genealogy Society, which has been handling negotiations with the city, were not present at the council meeting that endorsed the new parks ordinance. But the gallery was packed with supporters of the Carverys — some from Africville, others not.

Alderman Larry Uteck was quick to point out the society's absence, asking: "Are we dealing with an organization that represents the Africville descendants or are we not?"

Some blacks in the audience blamed "divide and conquer" tactics for the apparent rift. And those tactics prevailed during the 1960s relocation of Africville, weakening the community's resolve to remain intact.

There are times, however, when a group can divide and conquer itself, with tragic results. Hopefully, that is not happening to the people of Africville today.

A year later, the Africville compensation committee continued its pressure on the city.

Abused stepchild seeks compensation
April 28, 1996

Africville has always been Halifax's abused stepchild. Unlike Cinderella, however, Africville didn't make it to the ball and never got a chance to try on the glass slippers. There have been plenty of wicked witches in the Africville story, but few fairy godmothers. And now the clock is about to strike midnight — not at the prince's ball, but in a Nova Scotia courtroom.

The Africville Genealogy Society and other former residents of the small, predominantly black community that was bulldozed 30 years ago are seeking an order from the Supreme Court of Nova Scotia that would compel Halifax to sell the land on which Africville once stood — part of which is now Seaview Park — and pay the residents the value of their interest. A law firm from Kentville is handling their case.

The courts will be the arena in which lawyers will contest conflicting views of history: Africville's and that of what was once the City of Halifax.

Africville had existed for more than a century before the destruction of its buildings and relocation of its residents. Although the professed purpose for its removal was to make way for the approach to the MacKay Bridge, the real motivations had nothing to do with the bridge or any other form of "industrial development."

Long before the first house came down in a process that took the better part of a decade, Africville had been portrayed in the media and perceived by the public as a "slum," a "ghetto," an "eyesore," an "embarrassment." Anyone who defended the community was either ignored or shouted down, and Africville residents' desire to remain where they were was condescendingly dismissed as "fear of integration."

The city's position was — and still is — that the relocation was done in the best interests of Africville's people and the compensation paid to its residents was fair. That view was reinforced by an astonishingly self-serving report the city released in 1994, which not only called the compensation the residents received "generous," but also suggested that their memories of life in Africville were little more than a nostalgic "myth." The report also reinforced the notion that the relocation was a high-minded attempt to alleviate poverty and eradicate segregation.

In a way, the lawsuit is the Africville residents' reply to the city's report. For them, the relocation represented the final chapter in a history of neglect and abuse that dated back almost to Africville's beginnings in the early 19th century.

It is well known that although they paid taxes like everyone else, Africville residents did not have water or sewer services. They had to make do with wells, which, according to the lawsuit, "became contaminated and polluted and caused the (residents) to suffer health problems."

However, Halifax had no qualms about locating other, less beneficial facilities in or near Africville, including: a slaughterhouse; a prison; a "night-soil" disposal pit; a railroad line running through the community; an infectious-diseases hospital; a garbage dump and incinerator

The dump, opened in 1947, was particularly galling to Africville residents because for outsiders it defined their community. More than a few ignorant souls actually believed the community had been built next to the dump when in fact Africville was settled more than 100 years before the landfill was opened.

Why did Africville receive noxious facilities no one else wanted, but not water or sewer services? Because the community was black, and therefore considered inferior and powerless to prevent the city from doing whatever it wanted.

During the debate that began when Africville residents asked for compensation similar to what Sackville residents are receiving for a landfill that is still in operation, attempts were made to belittle Africville's concerns. The nay-sayers pointed out that Sackville was not a black community, but it received a landfill against its wishes just the same.

Other white communities had railroad tracks running through them or prisons and slaughterhouses next door. And a white community called Greenbank was demolished to make way for private development.

But what white community had all these things happen to it at once? That's the difference. That's where racism enters the discussion.

Negotiations between the Africville Genealogy Society and Halifax over the society's demand for either a return of Africville's land to its residents and their descendants, or fair compensation for its loss have been dragging for years. At one point, the city offered the society a $100,000 scholarship fund for former residents and a parcel of land for the construction of a replica of the community's Seaview Baptist Church. As far back as 1992, the province pledged $200,000 toward the construction of the replica.

But the replica remains unbuilt, amid wrangling over further funding and the availability of water and sewer service — an old story in Africville.

And now the players in the game have changed. The City of Halifax is no more; it is now part of the amalgamated entity known as the Halifax Regional Municipality. Unwilling to risk the possibility of being lost in the minutiae of post-merger politics, the Africville Genealogy Society has taken its cause to the courts.

Halifax's black stepchild is still knocking on the palace door. And at the stroke of a judge's gavel, the city just might turn into a pumpkin.

Someday, there'll be Africville justice
July 21, 1996

This week, Africville celebrates its annual reunion. This year, the displaced black community took a major step toward the righting of a wrong done more than 30 years ago.

Seaview Park is where the houses of Africville once stood, and it's where the community's former residents have gathered since 1985 to remember what they still call "up home." People who were only children when bulldozers tore down their houses in the 1960s consider Africville home, as do teenagers and 20-somethings who were born after the last Africville resident, Aaron "Pa" Carvery, departed in 1970.

For several years the Africville Genealogy Society, which represents former community residents and their descendants, has been negotiating with Halifax to gain equitable compensation for the loss of their home and to regain use of the land that was once their property. The city's strategy could be summed up in three words: stall, stall, stall. It's a battle of attrition: keep delaying until the other side gives up and goes away.

Even a partial deal that would have established a scholarship fund for Africville descendants and provided land for the long-promised Seaview Baptist Church replica has been tangled in red tape for the past two years.

In the meantime, a "live-in" protest that former residents Eddie and Victor Carvery began back in 1994 continues. At that time, the Carvery brothers set up camp in Seaview Park and vowed to remain until Africville residents received proper compensation for their losses.

Last year, Halifax passed an anti-camping bylaw intended to force the Carverys to leave. They responded by moving their camper and tent to a part of Seaview Park not owned by the city.

Earlier this year, Victor Carvery was charged with making threats after an altercation with workers from an environmental company and a municipal employee. Carvery pleaded not guilty and will stand trial in January.

The Carverys' protest has been the most visible aspect of Africville residents' dissatisfaction. With the amalgamation of Halifax, Dartmouth, Bedford and Halifax County into a "supercity" earlier this year, it appeared that Africville might have become lost in a myriad of other merger matters. In April, the Africville Genealogy Society took its case off the municipal treadmill and filed a lawsuit against Halifax with the Nova Scotia Supreme Court.

The suit asks the court to order Halifax to sell the land on which the community of Africville once stood and pay the former residents current interest value. To support the request, the Genealogy Society's lawyers provided a litany of legal arguments that summed up Africville's grievances:

The city failed to provide water and sewer services for the community, then used the lack of those services as justification to relocate the residents.

The city placed unwanted, noxious facilities such as an infectious diseases hospital and a garbage dump in or near the community.

The city "threatened, pressured and forced" residents to accept inadequate compensation for their property during the relocation.

After the relocation, the city failed to live up to its promises of benefits and opportunities for displaced residents. The suit also claims damages for pain and suffering, fraud, deceit, bad faith, breach of contract, destruction of property, conspiracy, and intimidation. It embodies 30 years of frustration and unfinished business.

Predictably, the supercity struck back — in a particularly underhanded fashion. Not long after the Genealogy Society launched its suit, municipal lawyers filed a "demand for particulars" from the plaintiffs.

The "particulars" involve specific, detailed information about the former Africville residents and descendants, such as the "true value" of their properties; the names of city officials who may have been involved in the alleged intimidation of residents during the relocation and the sites of wells the plaintiffs say were polluted.

Ironically, the Genealogy Society had been seeking that very information during its negotiations with Halifax. But Irvine Carvery, who was recently replaced as president of the society by George Grant, said they were told the information was "confidential."

"And here they have their legal team requesting that information from us," he told *The Daily News* last month.

The supercity's gambit indicates that the courts will be just as difficult a battleground as city hall. Delays and stalling will continue. But at least the courts cannot delay the matter indefinitely. Somewhere down the road, though the journey may take months or years, Africville's legal odyssey will be over. And the community may even find justice at the end of that road. In the meantime, Africville and its friends continue to get together "up home" once a year.

The Africville waiting game goes on ... and on ... and on
July 27, 1997

The last weekend of July is Africville's time. Every year in the middle of the summer, Seaview Park becomes what it used to be: Africville, a historically black community that lasted more than a century before its houses and church were bulldozed during the 1960s.

Africville residents, descendants and friends gather at the Bedford Basin to remember what they once had. They set up campers where their houses once stood, and a big green tent takes the place of the old Seaview Baptist Church.

The social planners who authorized that destruction believed the people of Africville would eventually be absorbed into the larger Halifax community and memories of their original home — and the manner of its passing — would fade.

Some residents did blend smoothly into what is now the Halifax Regional Municipality. Others had difficulty. Either way, the memories didn't fade.

Over the past two years, Africville issues have simmered like a pot on a back burner turned down to the lowest heat level. The waiting game continues. The authorities who hold Africville's fate in their hands believe time is their ally. But they are as wrong about that now as they were in the 1960s. Time has no effect on the spirit of a community that refuses to die.

Also, time can heal wounds — or open them wider.

The darkness-at-dawn destruction of the Seaview Church, the heart and soul of the old Africville community, inflicted one of the worst wounds on residents already reeling from the effects of imminent relocation. In 1991, the provincial government announced that a replica of the Seaview Church would be erected on its former site in the park. The church replica would house the Africville: A Spirit That Lives On exhibit that toured Canada several years ago. The government said it would provide funding for the project, and the Africville Genealogy Society said it would launch a fund-raising drive of its own.

The replica remains only a promise. Even the parcel of land the old City of Halifax had promised for the replica remains stuck in red tape.

Obviously, the reincarnation of the Seaview Church is off the radar screen of the amalgamated city's beleaguered government. Will newly installed Premier Russell MacLellan keep a promise made five years ago by a different government? Or will the waiting game continue?

But then, some Africville residents know how to play that game. After the 1994 reunion, two brothers — Eddie and Victor Carvery — decided they weren't going to leave. They set up a camp and said they would remain until compensation beyond the deals made in the '60s was provided for the people who lost their land.

The city tried to chase them out with an anti-camping bylaw, but the Carvery brothers simply moved their camper and tent to a part of the park the city doesn't own.

Earlier this year, Victor Carvery received a year's probation for a 1996 incident at the park. The brothers continue their waiting game.

On another front, the waiting is guaranteed to go on for years. Tired of endless negotiations, the Africville Genealogy Society filed a lawsuit against Halifax with the Nova Scotia Supreme Court in 1996. The suit asked the court to force the city to sell the former Africville land and pay current interest value to Africville residents.

The society's complaint reads like a compendium of Africville's grievances, past and present: failure to provide essential services such as water and sewers; placing a garbage dump in the community; use of threats to coerce residents to accept inadequate compensation for the loss of their property during relocation; failure to live up to post-relocation promises.

In response, the city's lawyers demanded "particulars" from the society detailed, specific information about the Africville residents and their claims. The city had earlier refused to provide that information to the Genealogy Society, saying it was "confidential."

The lawsuit stayed tied up throughout 1997. The waiting game continues.

If delays like this had occurred when the city made its decision to demolish Africville in the 1960s, the community would still be standing.

One day, the wrong done to Africville will be redressed. Until then, those who seek justice for the community will play the waiting game.

A site for sore eyes
August 2, 1998

For the past 15 years, the end of July has marked a week-long resurrection of a community that continues to live long after its houses and church were bulldozed out of existence. The community is Africville, and the event that winds up today is the annual reunion of former Africville residents, and their descendants and friends.

Seaview Park is where Africville once stood. During the reunion, the community stands again, with camper vehicles occupying old house sites and a large tent substituting for the old Seaview United Baptist Church.

This year's reunion bears special significance. It's the 150th anniversary of the first land purchase in the area. And it coincides with a visit to Halifax by Rosa Parks, who sparked the U.S. civil rights movement by refusing to give up her seat on a bus to a white passenger back in 1955. Parks is here to receive an honorary degree from Mount Saint Vincent University.

Beyond that, however, the reunion comes on the heels of a recent announcement from the Historic Sites and Monuments Board of Canada. The Africville location, along with the Little Dutch Church on Brunswick Street and Pier 21, a former immigration centre on the Halifax waterfront, has been accorded recognition by the board as places of national historic significance in the cultural communities category.

That acknowledgment stands in stark contrast to the negative images of Africville served up by the media during the years before the community's destruction. Back then, Africville was called an "eyesore." Now, it will be a site for sore eyes.

Unlike the Little Dutch Church or Pier 21, there are no material remnants of Africville at Seaview Park. A sundial with the names of Africville's founding families is the only indication — other than Victor and Eddie Carvery's four-year-old protest camp — that a community once existed on the park's grassy slopes; that people's lives were once lived there.

The Historic Sites Board's recognition of Africville's historic significance is yet another step along the road to atonement for the wrong that was done to the community back in the 1960s. But more steps need to be taken, and the foot-dragging characteristic of the past few years is continuing.

Many of the people displaced by the relocation believe they were not properly compensated for the land and homes they lost. In 1994, the issue resurfaced when the people of Sackville received compensation for the presence of a municipal landfill in their community. Africville residents, who had also been forced to endure a landfill, believed they deserved compensation as well.

As well, the city's purchase of Africville lands was called into question. The pre-amalgamation city of Halifax responded by issuing a report that said the land deals were not only fair, but in some cases generous.

That assessment infuriated more than a few Africville residents. Anger that had been suppressed for decades was vented during public meetings with city officials. Africville residents spoke of somehow getting the land back and rebuilding their community. The talk eventually became more than just a pipe dream.

In 1996, the Africville Genealogy Society filed a lawsuit that asked the Supreme Court of Nova Scotia to compel Halifax to sell the land on which Africville once stood, and pay former residents the value of their interest in the property. The case continues to drag through the justice system.

Another unresolved issue is the promise the provincial government made back in 1992 to build a replica of the Seaview Church, which would house the 1989 Africville exhibit that helped to put the community back on the map in a symbolic, if not a physical, sense. Since then, the replica has been snared in bureaucratic red tape, and has not yet been built.

The Historic Sites Board's recognition would have been even more meaningful if the replica were now standing as a monument to the pride and resilience of Africville's people. As the years drag on, the promise the government made to build it becomes hollower.

Still, patience and persistence will win the day for Africville, regardless of whether or not the church is rebuilt. There are greater matters to be resolved, such as the court case, which could have moral and legal significance similar to that of native land claims.

Opponents of Africville justice who believe a wait-it-out strategy of endless delay will thwart the community's aspirations should remember that the last people born in Africville will still be alive during the second half of the next century. And Africville's spirit will survive well beyond that time.

The lawsuit continues. The church replica remains unbuilt. The Carvery brothers continue their vigil. Africville's spirit lives on, and so does that of everyone who is Black and Bluenose.